HOW DO YOU SPELL . . . ?

Correct spelling is a necessary skill for anyone who writes—which means just about everyone. This essential guide, written in straightforward, easy-to-follow language, will teach you how to become the good speller you want to be. Complete with sections on troublesome letter combinations, tips on avoiding British and other ostentatious spellings, mnemonics, and writing and self-test exercises, the book will help you, in just 20 days, to eliminate forever such common confusions as:

- Whether to end a word with *-ance* or *-ence*; *-able* or *ible*; *-ary* or *-ery*; *-er* or *-or*; *-sy* or *-cy*.

- When to drop the final *e* before adding a suffix and when to retain it.

- How to choose among *-cede*, *-ceed*, and *-sede*; among *-ise*, *-ize*, and *-yze*; between *-ly* and *-ally*; between *-efy* and *-ify*.

- When a word is spelled *-ie* and when *-ei*.

NORMAN LEWIS has written a great many well-known and popular books on improving language skills, including *The New American Dictionary of Good English, Instant Word Power,* and *Thirty Days to Better English* (all available in Signet editions), as well as *Word Power Made Easy.* He taught for many years at the City College of New York and at New York University. He is now Professor of English at Rio Hondo College, in Whittier, California.

ALSO BY NORMAN LEWIS

See, Say, and Write! Books I, II

RSVP—Reading, Spelling, Vocabulary, Pronunciation, Books A, B; 1, 2, 3

RSVP for College English Power, Books I, II, III

RSVP with Etymology, Books 1, 2, 3

Instant Spelling Power for College Students

Instant Word Power

Rapid Vocabulary Builder, revised edition

Word Power Made Easy, revised edition

The New Roget's Thesaurus in Dictionary Form, revised edtion

How to Read Better and Faster, fourth edition

Thirty Days to a More Powerful Vocabulary (with Wilfred Funk), revised edition

The Modern Thesaurus of Synonyms

The New Power with Words

Thirty Days to Better English

How to Become a Better Reader

New Guide to Word Power

Dictionary of Modern Pronunciation

Correct Spelling Made Easy

Dictionary of Correct Spelling

Better English

New American Dictionary of Good English

How to Get More Out of Your Reading

How to Speak Better English

The Lewis English Refresher and Vocabulary Builder

Power with Words

20 DAYS TO BETTER SPELLING

by
Norman Lewis

A SIGNET BOOK

NEW AMERICAN LIBRARY

SIGNET TRADEMARK REG. U.S. PAT. OFF. AND FOREIGN COUNTRIES
REGISTERED TRADEMARK—MARCA REGISTRADA
HECHO EN DRESDEN, TN

SIGNET, SIGNET CLASSIC, MENTOR, ONYX, PLUME, MERIDIAN
and NAL BOOKS are published by NAL PENGUIN INC.,
1633 Broadway, New York, New York 10019

First Signet Printing, February, 1989

1 2 3 4 5 6 7 8 9

PRINTED IN THE UNITED STATES OF AMERICA

Contents

Contents

Your 20-Day Program for Better Spelling

What This Book Can Do for You

English spelling is difficult—no one claims otherwise. But you will find that it is far from difficult to become an excellent speller.

———

Let me tell you this about English spelling—

It is, without a doubt, the most perplexing, most confusing, most paradoxical, most contradictory, and most frustrating system of putting letters together ever devised by man.

It is, indeed, exactly as the noted economist Thorstein Veblen once described it, probably in a moment of understandable exasperation—

"[It] satisfies," said Veblen, "all the requirements of the canons of reputability under the law of conspicuous waste. It is archaic, cumbrous, and ineffective."

It is the kind of system which caused Andrew Jackson, our seventh President, to make his famous remark, also, doubtless, in a moment of pique—

Said Jackson, "It's a damned poor mind that can think of only one way to spell a word!"

But it is the system under which we operate—and perplexing, confusing, contradictory, and frustrating though it may be, if accurate spelling is your goal you have no choice but to come to terms with it.

You *can* come to terms with English spelling.

Indeed, you can do more than that. You can attain a considerable degree of skill and self-assurance—you can perhaps even come very close to complete mastery.

You can do all this through an intensive, carefully set up, and comprehensive training program.

Thorough and successful training in English spelling is probably far easier to achieve than you may realize; the time required is probably far less than you expect.

Do you consider yourself an incorrigibly poor, a practically hopeless speller? Within a short time after you start your training the improvement can be tremendous, the results almost spectacular.

Or do you, like so many educated people, feel that there are certain specific weaknesses, certain special areas of doubt and confusion in your spelling? A short period of intensive training can transform you into as nearly perfect a speller as it is humanly possible to be.

To become an efficient and self-confident speller of English words requires no unusual memory power; no more than average education and literateness; no greater ability to concentrate than most people normally have; and no special talent or flair for language.

All you need is a sound approach, the proper kind of training, and a sincere willingness to devote time and effort.

The sound approach and proper training you will find in this book—

The time and effort are up to you.

———

AUTHOR'S NOTE: As a matter of convenience, *he*, *him*, and *his* are used in this book to refer to a person of *either* sex. *He/she*, *him/her*, and *his/her* are, to this writer, awkward and unnecessary—as most readers understand, *he*, *him*, and *his* indicate a *person*, not a *male*.

2

The Two Keynotes of Your Training Program

The broad base of your learning will involve a complete understanding of the fundamental principles under which English spelling operates, combined with an automatic adjustment, through memory-association devices, to the correct patterns of specially difficult demons.

———

This book aims, directly and primarily, to increase your spelling ability, to make you a far better, far more accurate speller, to eliminate most, if not all, of your *unconscious* errors, and to help you settle your doubts and confusions about commonly misspelled words.

But of perhaps even greater importance, this book offers you a special psychological dividend—

A dividend that comes from a rich and rewarding learning experience in a field where many people—perhaps you are among them—have had only failure and frustration—

A dividend that comes from a sound and intensive training program that will produce immediate and observable results.

For the *satisfaction* and *strong feeling of accomplishment* that result from successful training will play as effective a role in building your security and self-assurance in spelling as the training itself or the knowledge gained from such training.

Let me explain now, detail by detail and point by point, how this intensive training program sets up.

I. BASIC PRINCIPLES

Twenty-three main chapters in the book will discuss—slowly, methodically, clearly—the fundamental principles under which English spelling operates.

The *explanations* of these dry-as-dust principles will be our least concern—for such explanations, by themselves, are of negligible value and can be read (in their characteristic dry-as-dust language) in the introductory pages of any large dictionary.

What these twenty-three chapters will give you, by means of techniques and methods to be explained shortly, is thorough and intensive training in *applying the principles* to the solution of the kind of problems that incessantly plague the average speller—

Problems like:

When to double a consonant, and when to leave it alone.

Whether to end a word with *-ance* or *-ence; -able* or *-ible; -ary* or *-ery; -er* or *-or; -sy* or *-cy*, etc.

When to drop a final *-e* before adding a suffix, and when to retain it.

When to write *-ie*, and when to write *-ei*.

How to choose between *-cede, -ceed,* and *-sede*; between *-ise, -ize,* and *-yze*; between *-ly* and *-ally*; between *-efy* and *-ify*, etc., etc.

These comparatively few but crucial and constantly recurring problems account for over 90 per cent of the errors commonly made by educated adults—and efficient training in the basic principles of English spelling can eliminate every one of them.

You will not, I repeat, merely learn these principles—

Rather, you will be thoroughly trained to apply them successfully to the solution of recurrent problems—

You will completely understand them in all their various aspects and ramifications—

You will realize what's behind them, why they function as they do, where the exceptions and inconsistencies and irregularities come from.

You will thus recognize that despite the seeming lawlessness of spelling patterns there are at bottom broad and pervading conventions which govern the proper sequence of letters in English words.

And, as an inevitable result of training in the application of basic principles, you will shortly be able to make instantaneous, unconfused, and accurate decisions as to the correct patterns of most of the words which may now trouble you.

II. MNEMONICS (pronounced *ne-MON-iks*)

The *word* "mnemonics" may be new to you; but the *idea* behind the word is probably quite familiar.

Mnemonics are special aids to memory, memory tricks if you like, based on the theory of association.

It would be difficult and tiresome, for example, to memorize the exact number of days in every one of the twelve months—but the well-known rhyme *"30 days hath September, etc."* eliminates the need for painful and perhaps untrustworthy memorizing. The rhyme itself can be learned in a few seconds—and with the *mnemonic* in mind you can know instantaneously and correctly whether a month has 28, 30, or 31 days.

It would be equally tiresome to commit to memory the direction of the one-way traffic on each of the hundred-odd streets in New York City. So most New York motorists use a simple and effective *mnemonic: even*-numbered streets go *east*. The initial *e*'s in *even* and *east* form an association device for quick and accurate remembering—in other words, a *mnemonic*.

Fifty-five special spelling demons, words that are particularly confusing even to the most literate of spellers (such as *embarassed* or *embarrassed?*, *anoint* or *annoint?*, *inoculate* or *innoculate?*, *dependant* or *dependent?*, *battalion* or *batallion?*, etc.), are discussed in the ten mnemonics chapters[1] of the book, each demon tied up to some sort of association device so that its correct pattern can be learned—permanently and unforgettably—in a few seconds.

The mnemonic for *embarrassed*, for example, is "two robbers were *embarrassed* in Sing Sing." The important problem in *embarrassed* is the number of *r*'s and *s*'s—the mnemonic (two robbers, Sing Sing) immediately and clearly demands two of each.

The mnemonic for *inoculate* is its synonym *inject*. The problem of how many *n*'s and *c*'s is settled at once—as in *inject*, only one of each.

The confusing problem of *batallion* or *battalion* is solved quickly by using the related word *battle* as a mnemonic. Like *battle*, *battalion* has two *t*'s and one *l*.

Your training in mnemonics will give you immediate and effortless control over the most frequently misspelled words in the English language. Five to ten of these words will be presented in each mnemonics chapter, and constant and repeated review of past demons and their association links in each succeeding mnemonics chapter will eventually make the correct pattern of these fifty-five troublesome forms practically automatic in your writing.

You will be highly conscious of the mnemonic for each word only through the period of your training. The first half-dozen times you write *embarrassed, inoculate, battalion* or any of the other fifty-five demons, you will pause and say the mnemonic to yourself. After that first half-dozen times, you will be ready to give up the association devices as *conscious* aids. Then the mnemonics will begin to fade from your conscious thinking, for the correct patterns of the confusing words you have studied will have become a permanent part of your self-assured spelling reactions—

—As self-assured and lacking in doubt or hesitation as the patterns of simple forms like *cat* or *school* or *night* or *girl* or any other words which you now write correctly without second thought.

---

[1]These are inserted at random after various basic-principles chapters.

Two Special Techniques in Your Training

The success of your work with this book will depend on your use of the two indispensable techniques that train you to become *visually* and *muscularly* adjusted to correct spelling patterns. These techniques will make your new spelling habits permanent and automatic.

———

Learning is a complex activity.

It is of course basically intellectual, and in fields like mathematics, or literature, or English grammar, the purely intellectual processes are the predominating if not the exclusive factors to be reckoned with.

But other factors are also involved in many types of learning.

In learning to speak a foreign language, you have to develop a certain facility in the physical organs of speech in order to be able to reproduce the required accent; in learning a comparatively simple skill like typing or a fairly difficult one like surgery you must develop a high degree of manual dexterity; in learning to drive an automobile you must develop habits of instantaneous muscular responses, etc.

Foreign languages, typing, surgery, driving a motorcar—these are all real learning situations, and although intellectual development is at the base of each, there is still a good deal of physical or bodily learning that must go on before genuine skill can be acquired.

So also in spelling.

The foundation of mastering correct spelling patterns is of course intellectual—and this intellectual foundation will be emphasized by your training in basic principles and in the use of mnemonics.

But the attainment of genuine skill and self-assurance in spelling also requires a certain amount of visual and muscular re-education. Let me explain these two special techniques in your training.

I. SHARPENING YOUR VISUAL MEMORY

Visual memory is part of the human equipment—it is perhaps better developed in some people than in others, but every normal human being has a good, serviceable visual memory.

Your visual memory is a storehouse of familiar images. Owing to visual memory, you can recognize something or somebody you've previously seen without carefully examining every detail, you can instantaneously react to familiar words on a page of print without looking at every letter, you can immediately distinguish your wife from your mother-in-law without engaging in a feature-by-feature analysis, etc.

Visual memory for spelling patterns develops by itself over the years—but it is often a slow and long process. And all too frequently it does not grow in precisely the direction that is most helpful.

If in the course of your training program with this book you discover X words which you never realized you were misspelling, plus Y words which you were never really sure of, then there are at least X plus Y instances in which your visual memory did not cooperate with your needs. These X plus Y words probably came up in your reading with a certain frequency—but because, as is perfectly natural, you read for meaning and not for patterns, you saw the correct spellings but never formed a sufficiently strong visual impression to be able to reproduce the words accurately and confidently.

A very important part of your training, then, will be devoted to sharpening your visual memory of spelling patterns by showing you how to react strongly to the appearance of the crucial letters or areas in certain words— the letters that cause the most confusion, the areas where many spellers are tempted into error.

The crucial letters or areas of every troublesome word throughout the book will be printed in heavy black type, thus: super**sede**, ex**ceed**, ni**e**ce, se**i**ze, occu**rrence**, etc.

Examine each such word carefully, staring at it for several seconds.

Pay particular attention to the heavy black letters— these are the letters with which you will aim to gain the greatest visual intimacy, so that eventually any other combinations will look awkward, out-of-balance, and therefore unquestionably incorrect.

Now conceal the word with a card or a slip of paper and attempt to reproduce the correct pattern on the blank line to the right; then expose the word and compare what you have written with the printed pattern.

If your answer is in error, correct it. (Old habits die hard, but one can learn from one's mistakes, as any child who has touched a hot stove will tell you.)

Such visual emphasis will start an unusual chain of circumstances. After carefully examining the exact pattern of a troublesome word for a few seconds, you will be involuntarily on the alert for it in all your reading; and you will probably be somewhat startled to notice how often it occurs, how strongly it arrests the eye. Every time you meet it you will again be observing its correct spelling pattern, again driving a little deeper than before your visual adjustment to its proper appearance and especially to the correct combination of letters in its crucial area.

II. SHARPENING YOUR MUSCULAR
OR "KINESTHETIC" MEMORY

In addition to your visual memory, your muscular or, as it is called technically, *kinesthetic* memory is an important factor in your mastery of English spelling.

Kinesthetic memory, like visual memory, is part of the human equipment. It is a storehouse of previous muscular activity and is well developed in every normal human being.

It is your kinesthetic memory that permits you to bring a glass to your lips without conscious direction from your brain. It is your kinesthetic memory that regulates more complex muscular activity such as that involved in typing, swimming, driving a car, catching a ball, performing a surgical operation or writing a word correctly.

But all these activities had to be slowly learned and, at first, consciously directed by the brain. When a muscular response has been performed frequently enough, the muscles seem to do their own thinking—no conscious direction is required from the brain; the act has become reflexive and automatic.

By far the greatest proportion of words you now write are the result of automatic kinesthetic memory—you rarely stop on familiar, easily spelled words to figure out which letter comes after which.

But because it is so easy today, don't think it just happened. As a child you learned very carefully and consciously to write *cat* and *rat* and *night* and *light*—now the reaction is so customary that it has become automatic, your muscles respond as if of their own volition, almost as reflexively as in eating or swallowing or walking or raising your arm to ward off a blow.

In successful training, you will wish to store up in your kinesthetic memory the correct spelling patterns of all the troublesome and confusing words you meet, so that accurate muscular reactions eventually become as automatic as in writing the simple, easily spelled words you now know so well.

This, too, will not happen by itself—you will have to train for it.

Two Special Techniques in Your Training

Your kinesthetic training will go hand in hand with your visual training. Every time you examine a word, conceal it, and then write it in the blank line, your muscles will be guided by the visual image your mind has retained, and you will begin to store up correct patterns in your kinesthetic memory.

You will find an opportunity to make a kinesthetic adjustment to the spelling pattern of every important word at least two and often three or more times within a single chapter. *Take advantage of every such opportunity.*

Your training program, then, takes three essential approaches to the development of a high order of skill in spelling:

1. *Intellectual:* Full understanding of fundamental principles combined with effective mnemonics for specially confusing words. This is the broad base of your training.

2. *Visual:* Thorough familiarity with the proper appearance of a word, with special emphasis on crucial letters.

3. *Kinesthetic:* Development of accurate and automatic muscular responses through the actual writing of a word a calculated number of times.

When you have made a full intellectual, visual, and kinesthetic adjustment, in that order, to the correct pattern of a troublesome word, the chances of your ever misspelling it through either carelessness or confusion will be practically negligible.

4

How to Use This Book
to Best Advantage

You are almost ready, now, to start your training. Here
are five important suggestions for making the time you
spend in such training pay big dividends.

Let me repeat, for emphasis, something I have said in
a previous chapter.

Namely, *that this training program on which you are
about to embark can be a rich and rewarding learning
experience.*

It can be rich and rewarding, it can give you a definite
feeling of accomplishment, it can offer you a good deal of
satisfaction and even pleasure—if you are willing to co-
operate with it.

Let me, therefore, make some suggestions that will
help you co-operate fully with the training this book
offers, that will make it possible for you to gain a maximum of benefit and improvement.

SUGGESTIONS FOR GETTING
THE MOST OUT OF THIS BOOK

1. *This is an intensive training program—so, for best
results, work intensively at it.*

"Intensively" would mean, in respect to time, *between a half hour and an hour a day*, and as many days in the week as the circumstances of your life permit.

This schedule will make it possible for you to master the twenty-seven training and ten mnemonic chapters of the book in no more than *twenty actual working days*—less than a month from start to finish if you actively commit yourself to a program of at least five days a week.

Thirty minutes to an hour a day for only twenty days may sound like a phenomenally short period in which to develop into an efficient, self-assured, and accurate speller, but that is all the time you will need to become fully trained—provided you work intensively, carefully, patiently.

For personal reasons of your own, you may prefer to take a longer period or you may, on the other hand, find it possible to complete the program in less than twenty working days. That is of course up to you. To provide a reasonable and attainable goal, I have indicated throughout the book which chapters can comfortably be completed in each day of your training—but if you prefer to set up a time schedule better suited to your needs, by all means do so. *In any case, however, whether you follow the program I offer or the one you plan for yourself, make every effort to keep to your training methodically and as much as possible without interruptions or extensive time gaps.*

2. Go slow.

I have tried to keep the style of the book clear, light, and breezy—and so you may be tempted into quick and superficial reading. Keep in mind, however, that this is a book only in the physical sense. In actuality, it is not a book at all, but a training program, a classroom on paper; for maximum benefit, work slowly on every page, digest the material thoroughly, make sure you fully understand and can successfully apply all the material in one chapter before you go on to the next.

You will notice, as you proceed with your training, a

good deal of calculated repetition, a deliberate step-by-step pace, constant summaries and recapitulations, and chance after chance to stop and practice. Suit your tempo to the demands of the program.

3. *Do not neglect to write each word as often as required.*

I have already explained the supreme importance of sharpening your visual and kinesthetic memory. To be a self-confident, accurate speller you need trained eyes and fingers as well as a trained mind. So keep a pen or pencil handy during all your sessions—and use it frequently. The more active a role you play, the more permanent your training will be.

4. *Take all tests as if in actual test situations.*

There are thirty-two chapter-end tests and four comprehensive review tests. To make self-checking simple and convenient, the answer to each question on all tests appears in parentheses directly to the right of the question. *Keep all answers concealed until you are ready to score the complete test.*

Take every test, and take it honestly. These test will provide you with objective, unbiased reports on your progress. And study your results—if they are poor you are not working conscientiously enough. Allow for normal human frailty, of course—an occasional error here and there will be of no great significance. But consistently low scores on the tests will indicate the need for careful review of past material and a firm resolve to proceed more cautiously on new material.

5. *Do not skip around; do not dip in casually or at random.*

This is a training book, not a reading book. No matter how good a speller you consider yourself, you may find surprises on every page; you may discover that you were making errors you never realized. If you are firmly convinced that you are an expert on the material of a particular chapter, turn to the test to make sure. Only a perfect score would indicate that the chapter can be safely skipped.

All right—that gives you all the briefing you need.

These four chapters of lengthy but necessary introduction may have made the attainment of complete spelling efficiency and security seem to require effort and tenacity.

Perhaps it does—but the dividends will be well worth the investment.

You provide the time, the tenacity, and the effort—this book will do the rest.

NOTE

Often, the blank line following a word will not be long enough for you to fill in the complete word. In such instances, you may wish to write the word on a separate sheet of paper. Possibly, you may prefer to do all your writing practice on paper instead of in the book.

5

How to Decide Between *-cede, -ceed* and *-sede*

PROBLEM

super**cede**, super**ceed**, *or* super**sede**?

SOLUTION

The problem of this chapter highlights the kind of troublesome and confusing dilemma that so often confronts the speller of English words.

It is typical of the vexatious decisions that have to be made so frequently in even the most informal of writing.

But like most other spelling problems, it can be solved quickly and easily—once you understand and learn to apply basic principles.

So let us examine the simple facts and basic principles behind the spelling patterns of all the English words that end in the pronunciation *seed*.

There are exactly a dozen such words, eleven of them in common use, the twelfth somewhat obscure—all of them with final syllables that are pronounced identically but spelled in three different ways: *-cede, -ceed,* or *-sede*.

To avoid doubt and confusion, to be able to make an instantaneous, self-assured, and accurate decision on the spelling of any word whose final syllable is pronounced *seed*, you have to know two facts.

How to Decide Between -cede, -ceed, and -sede

Fact 1

Of the twelve words, one, and only one, ends in the four letters -S-E-D-E.

That one word is:

super**sede** _____

Supersede, in fact, is the only word in the entire language with the -sede ending.

In short, *supersede* is unique.

And, as you will soon discover, unique spelling patterns are easy to remember. Because of their uniqueness, they stick in the mind like burs.

So you will have no further trouble with *supersede*.

How about the others?

You need be thoroughly familiar with three other words—three that are equally unique.

Fact 2

There are only three words in the language that end in the letters -C-E-E-D.

Namely:

suc**ceed** _____   pro**ceed** _____
ex**ceed** _____

These two facts, that only *supersede* ends in -sede and that only *succeed, proceed*, and *exceed* end in -ceed, permit you to make an immediate and correct choice between -sede, -ceed, and -cede.

For, obviously, with two of the three possible spellings accounted for, the eight remaining words of the original twelve can end in only one way: -C-E-D-E.

There is no point, of course, in your learning these eight words so completely that you can reel them off in alphabetical order. But examine each one for a few seconds and become visually and kinesthetically adjusted to its required pattern.

1. ac**cede** _____   3. **cede** _____
2. ante**cede** _____   4. con**cede** _____

5. inter**cede** _____   7. re**cede** _____
6. pre**cede** _____   8. se**cede** _____

How can you remember that *succeed, proceed,* and *exceed* belong in a class by themselves, and are not to be confused with the eight *-cede* words? How can you fix these three crucial verbs permanently in your mind, nail them down for all time?
Consider:

Succeed starts with *s.*

Proceed starts with *p,* and means *go ahead.* (The importance of the meaning will be evident in a moment.)

Exceed starts with *e.*

Now think of the key phrase, *Full Speed Ahead.*

This one phrase, *Full Speed Ahead,* and in particular the word *speed,* will be your guarantee against two unpleasant possibilities, to wit:

1. Any annoying doubt as to whether a word correctly ends in *-ceed* or *-cede.*

2. Any error in writing *-cede* for *-ceed,* or vice versa.

Notice how simply this mnemonic works:

Sp**eed** ends in **-eed**.
The **s** of speed identifies su**cceed**.
The **p** of speed identifies pro**ceed**.
The **e** of speed identifies ex**ceed**.
The ending of sp**eed** identifies the endings of all three words: su**cceed**, pro**ceed**, ex**ceed**.

And finally, the word *ahead* in *Full Speed Ahead* identifies *proceed,* which means *go ahead,* eliminates *precede,* which means *come before.*

Think of *Full Speed Ahead,* and you automatically write su**cceed**, **p**roceed and ex**ceed** with the correct *-ceed* ending, all other words (except, of course, *supersede*) with the correct *-cede* ending.

This may sound complicated until you are used to it. It is actually quite simple. As with all mnemonics, you will consciously think of *Full Speed Ahead* when you have occasion to write one of the three *-ceed* words—for a time. Eventually, the mnemonic will fade from your mind—when you have such automatic control over the *seed* verbs that key phrases are no longer necessary.

And that's all there is to the problem of making a choice between *-cede*, *-ceed*, and *-sede.*

Except for one noteworthy irregularity.

Proceed, as you know, belongs to one of the three *-ceed* verbs.

But the noun and adjective forms do not follow suit.

Contrary to what you might normally expect, these forms are spelled:

pro**ced**ure _____   pro**ced**ural _____

Which, as you will eventually learn to accept, is not surprising.

Because the most normal thing in English spelling is the unexpected.

Let us now gather our information and start to formulate basic principles.

Point 1

Only one word in English ends in *-sede*, namely *supersede.*

Point 2

Only three words in English end in *-ceed*, namely *succeed*, *proceed*, and *exceed*. (Key: *Full Speed Ahead.*)

Point 3

All other words of similar sound end in *-cede.*

Point 4

Procedure and *procedural*, however, do not follow the pattern of *proceed.*

TEST YOURSELF

I. Decide on the correct ending (*-cede*, *-ceed*, or *-sede*) that attaches to each of the following roots, then write the complete word with that ending. (It is most important to rewrite the word, not merely add the required ending; for only by this means can you gain the kinesthetic and visual practice so essential for making correct patterns reflexive and automatic.) For your convenience, the proper endings appear in parentheses along the right margin of the page—keep them concealed until you are ready to check your learning.

1. ac— _____ (cede)
2. con— _____ (cede)
3. suc— _____ (ceed)
4. se— _____ (cede)
5. pro— _____ (ceed)
6. pre— _____ (cede)
7. re— _____ (cede)
8. ante— _____ (cede)
9. ex— _____ (ceed)
10. super— _____ (sede)
11. inter— _____ (cede)

II. Decide on the missing letter or letters, then rewrite the complete word.

1. proc—dure _____ (e)
2. proc—dural _____ (e)
3. c—de _____ (e)
4. proc—d _____ (ee)
5. prec—de _____ (e)
6. conc—ding _____ (e)
7. sec—ding _____ (e)
8. super—ding _____ (se)
9. super—ded _____ (se)

10. ex—d _____ (cee)
11. ex—ding _____ (cee)
12. suc—ding _____ (cee)
13. inter—ding _____ (ce)
14. ac—ding _____ (ce)

A Footnote on Supersede

As you go on with your work in this book, it will soon become apparent that most of the peculiarities of English spelling are due to the mongrel ancestry of our language.

Almost every word you use was born in some foreign land—England, Italy, Greece, France, Germany, Norway, Denmark, India, China, Japan, Spain, etc.

And in most cases we retain the exotic spelling of the import, while Americanizing the pronunciation.

Hence the strange pattern of *supersede*, the only word in our language with the *-sede* ending.

Supersede was born in Rome thousands of years ago. It comes from Latin *super* above, and *sedeo*, to sit.

If one thing *supersedes* another, it figuratively, and by derivation, sits above it.

Supersede is the only verb in English that derives directly from Latin *sedeo*, to sit, hence the only word with the *-sede* termination. But many nouns and adjectives come *indirectly* from *sedeo* or one of its forms: *president*, one who sits before a group; *sedentary*, moving little, hence sitting, as in *sedentary occupation; session*, a sitting or meeting of a group of people; *sedate*, calm, hence sitting still, etc.

The eleven *-ceed* or *-cede* words in English, on the other hand, all derive ultimately from Latin *cedo*, go: *precede*, go or come before; *secede*, go away; *intercede*, go between; *proceed* go ahead, etc.

This doesn't explain why *succeed, proceed,* and *exceed* end in *-ceed* while the others end in *-cede*—and unfortunately there is no sound explanation. As our language grew, certain words became set in certain patterns—and those are the patterns, for better or worse, that we're stuck with today.

A Footnote on Antecede

Antecede is the one obscure verb in the list of common "seed" forms. It is practically never heard in speech nor seen in writing, but it does exist, and I have therefore felt compelled to include it in the complete list of *-cede* words.

Antecede, composed of Latin *ante*, before, and *cedo*, go, means *go before*—exactly the same as *precede*, which is the word in common use. The noun form, *antecedent*, is a grammatical term describing a word that *goes before* some pronoun, as in *the man who came to dinner. Man* is the antecedent of *who*.

I admit that this information is of little, if any, practical use—but take it for what it's worth.

(First Day, continued)

PRETEST

1. occu**rence,** occu**rrance,** *or* occu**rrence**?
2. superintend**ant** *or* superintend**ent**?
3. in**n**oculate, in**o**cculate, *or* in**o**culate?
4. indispens**ible** *or* indispens**able**?
5. depend**ible** *or* depend**able**?

MNEMONICS

1. (occu**rence,** occu**rrance,** *or* occu**rrence**?)

An effective mnemonic highlights the critical letters of a spelling demon, emphasizes the troublesome areas where the inefficient speller may be tempted into error. There are two problems in this word: (1) single or double *r*? (2) -*ence* or -*ance*? As soon as you realize that an OCCU**RRENCE** is a CU**RRENT** event, in a sense, you can conveniently solve both problems with a single mnemonic. CU**RRENT** is rarely if ever misspelled—if you can spell CU**RRENT** you can spell OCCU**RRENCE,** which has the same double *r* followed by *e*.

> *Correct spelling:* occu**rrence** _____
> *Mnemonic:* cu**rrent** event

2. (superintend**ant** *or* superintend**ent**?)

The troublesome area here is the final syllable: -*ant* or

-ent? In an apart**ment** house, why does the SUPERIN-
TEND**ENT** come around to the front door on the first of
every month? For the R**ENT** of course—and R**ENT** is
the mnemonic that shows you the required ending.

> *Correct spelling:* superintend**ent** _____
> *Mnemonic:*   r**ent**

3. (in**n**oculate, ino**cc**ulate, *or* inoculate?)

As you can begin to see, one of the frequent decisions
you have to make when you spell English words is whether
to double a consonant or leave it alone. Here the important questions are: Single or double *n*? And single or
double *c*?

The common misspelling contains, erroneously, either
two *n*'s or two *c*'s and, as it happens, the correct pattern
requires only one of each. An effective and easily remembered mnemonic should have some relation in meaning to the problem word, as well as highlighting the areas
of difficulty. To gain complete control over in**o**culate,
think of its synonym, in**je**ct, which, like in**o**culate, has
only one *c* and one *n*.

> *Correct spelling:* in**o**culate _____
> *Mnemonic:*   in**je**ct

4. (indispens**ible** *or* indispens**able**?)
5. (depend**ible,** *or* depend**able**?)

We have begun to attack some of the fundamental and
constantly recurring problems in English spelling. Whether
to end a word with *-ence* or *-ance*, whether to double a
consonant or leave it alone, whether to use the suffix
-able or *-ible*—these three are high, very high, on the list
of decisions you have to make over and over again in a
normal day of writing or typing. Eventually we shall
explore, and you will finally master, every aspect and
facet of these and other important problems. Meanwhile
we need a quick mnemonic for these two frequently
misspelled words. Realize that **able** workers are ordinarily
both depend**able** and indispens**able**, and your decision
can become an automatic one—both words end in *-able*.

Correct spelling: indispens**able** _____
depend**able** _____
Mnemonic: **Able** workers are depend**able**
and indispens**able**.

MNEMONICS CHART
Correct Pattern   Mnemonic

1. occu**rrence** _____ cu**rrent** event
2. superintend**ent** _____ **rent**
3. in**oculate** _____ in**ject**
4. indispens**able** _____ **able** worker
5. depend**able** _____ **able** worker

A Footnote on Indispensable

Indispensable is far more often misspelled than its cousin *dependable*—indeed, it is the rare speller who writes *-able* after *indispens-* and is self-confident enough to think no further about it. And there is good and sound reason for this confusion—most English words with a root ending in *-ns* take the suffix *-ible; defensible, reprehensible, incomprehensible*, etc. But not *indispensable*, nor, of course, its affirmative form, *dispensable*.

While *dependable* is nowhere nearly so often misspelled, I have purposely included it in the same chapter with *indispensable* so that you can link the two words in your mind—*dependable* will help you remember *indispensable*.

Consider one more point.

Some few spellers tend to write ind**espens**- instead of the correct ind**ispens**-. If you have, or think you may have, such a tendency, think of the related word *dispense*, which is practically never misspelled.

TEST YOURSELF

I. Check the correct pattern.
   1. (a) dependible,   (b) dependable   (b)
   2. (a) occurrence,   (b) occurrance   (a)
   3. (a) superintendant, (b) superintendent (b)

35

4. (a) indispensible,   (b) indispensable   (b)
5. (a) inoculate,   (b) innoculate   (a)

II. Recall the mnemonic for each word.
  1. occu**rrence** _____(**current** event)
  2. superintend**ent** _____   (**rent**)
  3. in**o**culate _____   (**inj**ect)
  4. indispens**able** _____ (**able** worker)
  5. depend**able** _____ (**able** worker)

III. Decide on the missing crucial letter or letters, then rewrite the complete word.
  1. depend—ble _____ (a)
  2. occu—nce _____ (rre)
  3. superintend—nt _____ (e)
  4. indispens—ble _____ (a)
  5. i—o—ulate _____ (n,c)

How to Decide Between
-ize, *-ise*, and *-yze*

PROBLEMS

anal**ize** *or* anal**yze**?
improv**ize** *or* improv**ise**?
surpr**ize** *or* surpr**ise**?
ostrac**ize** *or* ostrac**ise**?

SOLUTION

Good spelling is in a large part dependent on visual memory, as I have said. If, by now, *supersede* at first glance looks familiar and proper to you while *supercede* or *superceed* looks odd and improper, then you have begun to rely on your visual memory.

Everyone has a visual memory. You have one—and it is probably well developed, as it is in most human beings.

You rely on your visual memory every day—by means of it you can distinguish between Uncle Egbert and Aunt Lizzie, between a bowl of mush and a porterhouse steak, between a kiddie car and a Cadillac convertible. The things I have mentioned contain gross differences and are easy to distinguish one from the other—but things which contain fine and minute differences are just as easy to distinguish.

For example, playing cards.

If you devote any time to card games, you are constantly sharpening your visual memory of the fine differences between, say, a king and queen of diamonds, or an ace of clubs, and an ace of spades. When you pick up your hand for a bridge or canasta game you recognize the cards instantaneously and automatically, and you sort them out in whatever way is proper.

Sharpening, and learning to rely on, your visual memory is a basic and indispensable technique in the mastery of English spelling.

When you have sharpened your visual memory—

When you have learned to rely on visual memory to conquer certain confusing and easily misspelled words—

Then, without the slightest hesitation, you will be able to distinguish—instantaneously—a correct pattern from an incorrect pattern.

And you will be impelled—automatically—to accept the proper combination, to reject an improper one.

Most of your success in spelling today comes from an unconscious dependence on visual memory—which is as it should be. Visual memory is so valuable and effective a technique that I am going to help you depend on it to a greater and greater degree; I am going to show you how to develop it into a skill of a very high order.

Visual memory will be your means of successful attack on the words in this chapter.

These words belong to a group that cause the kind of headache no aspirin can cure.

There are over 450 of them—words whose final syllables sound exactly alike, but which may end in one of three ways:

1. *-ise*
2. *-ize*
3. *-yze*

Your first goal is to know, by visual assurance and without hesitation, which of the three endings to tack on to any of the 450 words you may have occasion to use.

And your final goal is to be able to react instantaneously, automatically, and accurately with the correct ending when you write any word in this group.

Does this sound like too formidable a task, too much to ask of one human being?

Actually there's nothing to it—it is simplicity itself.

For a knowledge of a few clear and foolproof principles, when combined with a sharpened visual memory, will give you full and self-confident control over all 450 of these perplexing words.

Point 5

Most of these confusing words end in -*ize*, the popular American ending. If you are ever in any real doubt, -*ize* is probably the safe form to use.

For example:

agon**ize**	caps**ize**
mechan**ize**	character**ize**
apolog**ize**	hypnot**ize**
minim**ize**	philosoph**ize**
appet**ize**	idol**ize**
alphabet**ize**	apolog**ize**
popular**ize**	modern**ize**
memor**ize**	organ**ize**

Don't become too involved with these -*ize* words. There are over 400 of them, and you need only remember that the mathematical probability of -*ize* being the correct ending is therefore very great.

Point 6

Two and only two common words end in -*yze*.[1] These two are:

1. anal**yze** _____   2. paral**yze** _____

[1]There are a few other, highly technical, words that end in -*yze*, notably *dialyze, catalyze,* and *electrolyze*—but if you are sufficiently familiar with chemistry or physics to use these words you probably know how to spell them.

I repeat, only these two common words end in -yze—they are easy to remember and can at once be cleared out of the way.

Point 7

There are, finally, thirty-six common words that end in -ise. These are the words to become most intimate with. Be absolutely sure of these thirty-six, and of *analyze* and *paralyze*, and the problem vanishes—*all others end in -ize.*

Aha, you are thinking skeptically, how am I going to remember thirty-six words that end in -ise?

It is easier than it sounds.

To begin with, you spell many of them correctly now—for only a few of them are subject to frequent misspelling by literate citizens. That alone narrows the field considerably.

Futhermore, you are not planning to memorize them, but only to react to them visually, which is considerably simpler. You need never rattle off the thirty-six -ise words—your simple goal is to become visually familiar with them, so that an -ize ending on any of them looks improper and awkward.

And, finally, thirty of the thirty-six -ise words fall into natural groupings, so that only six are left in isolation.

Let us examine the thirty that fall into natural groupings.

Group I. Any Combination with "wise"

1. **wise** _____
2. side**wise** _____
3. other**wise** _____
4. like**wise** _____
5. contrari**wise** _____
   etc.

Group II. Any Combination Ending in "-vise"

6. ad**vise** _____
7. super**vise** _____
8. re**vise** _____
9. impro**vise** _____
10. de**vise** _____

(The reason here is that such words are built on the Latin root *visus*, to see.)

Group III. Any Combination Built on the Word "rise"
11. **rise** _____
12. moon**rise** _____
13. sun**rise** _____
14. up**rise** _____
15. a**rise** _____

Note, please, that it is not the letter *r* which demands -*ise*, as words like *characterize, memorize,* and *popularize* show. It is a combination built on the actual word "rise" that counts.

Group IV. Any Common Words Ending in "-prise"
16. enter**prise** _____
17. ap**prise** _____
18. re**prise** _____
19. sur**prise** _____
20. com**prise** _____

(The obvious exception, of course, is *prize* itself, or any word built on it, such as *underprize* or *overprize*.)

Group V. Three Words and Only Three Ending in "-mise"
21. sur**mise** _____
22. compro**mise** _____
23. de**mise** _____

Group VI. Five Special "-cise" Words
24. *exer***cise** _____
25. ex**cise** _____
26. exor**cise** _____
27. in**cise** _____
28. circum**cise** _____

(Note that there are only five special -*cise* words. Others, like *ostracize, criticize, italicize,* etc., end in -*cize*. The reason for the special spelling of these five is that each comes from a Latin root containing an *s—incisus, to cut*.)

Group VII. Two "guise" Words
29. **guise** _____
30. dis**guise** _____

These thirty, since they fall into groupings, will offer no real difficulty.

And, with thirty grouped, we have only six isolated -*ise* words to commit to visual memory.

These are:

31. advert**ise** _____   34. merchand**ise** _____
32. desp**ise** _____   35. franch**ise** _____
33. chast**ise** _____   36. enfranch**ise** _____

So to attack the problem efficiently, you will take three simple steps for quick and successful learning.

Step 1

Become visually familiar with the two common *-yze* words:

   1. anal**yze** _____   2. paral**yze** _____

Step 2

Study the thirty-six common *-ise* words, seeing them in groups, and gaining a strong visual impression of each one.

I. "-wise"
   1. **wise** _____   4. like**wise** _____
   2. side**wise** _____   5. contrari**wise** _____
   3. other**wise** _____

II. "-vise"
   6. ad**vise** _____   9. impro**vise** _____
   7. super**vise** _____   10. de**vise** _____
   8. re**vise** _____

III. "-rise"
   11. **rise** _____   14. up**rise** _____
   12. moon**rise** _____   15. a**rise** _____
   13. sun**rise** _____

IV. "-prise"
   16. enter**prise** _____   19. sur**prise** _____
   17. ap**prise** _____   20. com**prise** _____
   18. re**prise** _____

V. "-mise"
   21. sur**mise** _____   23. de**mise** _____
   22. compro**mise** _____

How to Decide Between *-ize*, *-ise*, and *-yze*

VI. "-cise"
24. exer**cise** _____
25. ex**cise** _____
26. exor**cise** _____
27. in**cise** _____
28. circum**cise** _____

VII. "-guise"
29. **guise** _____
30. dis**guise** _____

VIII. Others
31. adver**tise** _____
32. des**pise** _____
33. chas**tise** _____
34. merchan**dise** _____
35. franch**ise** _____
36. enfranch**ise** _____

Step 3

All others, and whenever in doubt, you will spell *-ize*.

That's all there is to it—I think you'll agree that it is simpler than it may have seemed at first.

TEST YOURSELF

Decide on the proper ending (*-ize, -ise* or *-yze*) for each of the following, then rewrite the complete word.

1. mechan— _____ (ize)
2. appet— _____ (ize)
3. critic— _____ (ize)
4. anal— _____ (yze)
5. paral— _____ (yze)
6. likew— _____ (ise)
7. adv— _____ (ise)
8. superv— _____ (ise)
9. rev— _____ (ise)
10. dev— _____ (ise)
11. Anglic— _____ (ize)
12. bapt— _____ (ize)
13. civil— _____ (ize)
14. ar— _____ (ise)
15. enterpr— _____ (ise)

16. appr— _____ (ise)
17. repr— _____ (ise)
18. surpr— _____ (ise)
19. compr— _____ (ise)
20. equal— _____ (ize)
21. general— _____ (ize)
22. moral— _____ (ize)
23. surm— _____ (ise)
24. comprom— _____ (ise)
25. dem— _____ (ise)
26. minim— _____ (ize)
27. legal— _____ (ize)
28. local— _____ (ize)
29. exerc— _____ (ise)
30. exc— _____ (ise)

A Footnote on Forms

Analyze and *paralyze*, you now know, end in *-yze*. You will then have no trouble with the noun forms of these verbs, for you keep the *y* in its proper place, and otherwise spell according to sound.

analysis _____ paralysis _____

The letter *y* falls right in place, also, in forms like psychoanalyze, psychoanalysis, psychoanalyst, psychoanalytic (all preferably written as solid words, not hyphenated), paralytic, etc.

Whenever you have some doubt about the spelling of a difficult word, consider whether there is not some other form of the same word which you are sure of. If you can find such a related form, your problem is settled—use a similar pattern for the hard work.

This is so valuable a technique that we shall use it over and over in our mnemonics chapters.

PRETEST

1. siege *or* seige?
2. sieze *or* seize?
3. batallion *or* battalion?
4. parallel *or* paralell?
5. fricassee *or* friccasee?

MNEMONICS

1. (siege *or* seige?)
2. (sieze *or* seize?)

One of the major problems in English spelling is how to make an accurate and self-assured choice between *ie* and *ei*.

In Chapters 8 and 9 we'll explore the question thoroughly, but at this point it will be interesting and instructive to consider the two contrasting and somewhat contradictory forms SIEGE and SEIZE.

(As you continue with your training, you will note how effectively the mind stores up contradictory spellings.)

A SIEGE is the surrounding of a fortified city by an enemy army—and therein lies our obvious mnemonic. An army lays SIEGE to, or BESIEGES, a CITY—the letter *i* in CITY reminds you to use *i* before E in SIEGE and BESIEGE.

On the other hand, it is common practice, in certain violent levels of society, to SEIZE one's enemy or adversary by the NECK—the vowel *e* in NECK reminds you to use *e* before *i* in SEIZE and SEIZURE.

I admit that this contrast is somewhat fanciful, as many mnemonics are—but because the phrases "SIEGE of a CITY" and "SEIZE by the NECK" present clear and striking pictures, the mnemonics, fanciful though they may be, are easy to remember and will provide valuable aids in keeping straight on the proper combinations in SIEGE, BESIEGE, SEIZE, and SEIZURE.

> *Correct spellings:*   siege _____
> besiege _____
> seize _____
> seizure _____
>
> *Mnemonics:*   besiege, or lay siege to, a city; seize by the neck.

3. (batallion *or* battalion?)

As we shall learn in a later mnemonics chapter, one of the simplest and most practical of association devices is to make a memory link between a perplexing form of a word and a form that virtually defies misspelling.

To settle once and forever the question of how many *t*'s and *l*'s occur in the word under discussion, link it to its easily spelled form BATTLE. Everyone can spell BATTLE—and BATTLE, with its obvious two *t*'s and one *l*, immediately shows the correct combination in BATTALION.

> *Correct Spelling:*   battalion _____
> *Mnemonic:*   battle

4. (paralell *or* parallel?)

Here we have another major spelling problem—when to double a consonant and when to leave it alone.

If you link the test word to the phrase "ALL tracks are PARALLEL," you will avoid any hesitation and doubts as to which *l* requires doubling—make sure that the word ALL appears in PARALLEL and your problem is automatically and correctly solved.

Correct Spelling: **parallel** _____
Mnemonic: **all** tracks are para**ll**el

5. (fri**c**a**s**see *or* fri**cc**asee?)

For this type of cooking, think of **CASSEROLE**, a word which does not tempt to misspelling. **FRICASSEE** can be made in a **CASSEROLE**, and, like **CASSEROLE**, has one *c*, two *s*'s.

Correct Spelling: fri**cass**ee _____
Mnemonic: **casse**role

_____

MNEMONICS CHART

Correct Pattern	Mnemonic
1. si**e**ge _____	lay si**e**ge to, or
2. besi**e**ge _____	besi**e**ge, a c**i**ty
3. s**ei**ze _____	s**ei**ze by the n**e**ck
4. bat**t**alion _____	bat**t**le
5. para**ll**el _____	**all** tracks are para**ll**el
6. fri**cass**ee _____	**casse**role

TEST YOURSELF

I. Check the correct pattern.

1. (a) siege,	(b) seige		(a)
2. (a) besiege,	(b) beseige		(a)
3. (a) sieze,	(b) seize		(b)
4. (a) siezure,	(b) seizure		(b)
5. (a) batallion,	(b) battalion		(b)
6. (a) parallel,	(b) paralell		(a)
7. (a) friccasee,	(b) fricassee		(b)

II. Recall the mnemonic for each word.

1. si**e**ge _____	(city)
2. besi**e**ge _____	(city)
3. s**ei**ze _____	(neck)
4. bat**t**alion _____	(battle)

5. parallel _____ (all tracks)
6. fricassee _____ (casserole)
7. superintendent _____ (rent)
8. inoculate _____ (inject)
9. indispensable _____ (able worker)
10. dependable _____ (able worker)
11. occurrence _____ (current event)

III. Decide on the missing crucial letters, then write the complete word.

1. indispens—ble _____ (a)
2. depend—ble _____ (a)
3. occu—nce _____ (rre)
4. i—o—ulate _____ (n,c)
5. superintend—nt _____ (e)
6. s—ge _____ (ie)
7. bes—ge _____ (ie)
8. s—ze _____ (ei)
9. ba—a—ion _____ (tt,l)
10. para—e— _____ (ll,l)
11. fri—a—ee _____ (c,ss)

How to Decide Between *mis-* and *miss-*, *dis-* and *diss-*

PROBLEMS

misspelling *or* mispelling?
mishapen *or* misshapen?
dissapear *or* disappear?
dissapoint *or* disappoint?
dissatisfaction *or* disatisfaction?

SOLUTION

Practically no literate speller writes *miss-* at the beginning of a word that correctly starts with *mis-*.

Somehow, in English, there is little temptation to double the *s* in this prefix.

On the contrary, the tendency is the other way around. Among a goodly proportion of spellers, a certain number of crucial words which correctly start with *miss-* are incorrectly written with a single *s*.

Six such words are particularly troublesome:

1. misspell _____
2. misstate _____
3. misspend _____
4. misstep _____
5. misspeak _____
5. misshape _____

The poor speller, humanly if not logically, is likely to omit one of the two required *s*'s in each of these words.

Why, in all logic, do we need that second *s*?
Consider:
The basic roots of these words are:

    1. spell   4. step
    2. state   5. speak
    3. spend   6. shape

And to this basic root, in each case, is added the negative prefix *mis-*, an old English form meaning *bad(ly)*, *wrong(ly)*, etc.
Thus:

    1. *mis-* + *s*pell = mis*s*pell: *spell wrongly*
    2. *mis-* + *s*tate = mis*s*tate: *state incorrectly*
    3. *mis-* + *s*pend = mis*s*pend: *spend unwisely*
    4. *mis-* + *s*tep = mis*s*tep: *bad step*
    5. *mis-* + *s*peak = mis*s*peak: *speak wrongly*
    6. *mis-* + *s*hape = mis*s*hape: *shape badly*

In short, then—
When a root word starts with *s*, such as *spelling* or *shapen*, the addition of the negative prefix *mis-* will result in a double *s; misspelling, misshapen*, etc.
Most root words to which the prefix *mis-* will be added do not start with *s*. Hence they will contain a single, not a double, *s*.
As in:

    mis- + apprehend = mi*s*apprehend
    mis- + take = mi*s*take
    mis- + hap (from happen) = mi*s*hap
    mis- + construe = mi*s*construe
        etc.

And some few words beginning with *miss-* are not built on a negative prefix, but contain a double *s* for some other reason. These words are rarely misspelled, however, and offer no problem. Merely to complete the record, I will list some common *miss-* words below, none of which contain a negative prefix.

missile
missing, etc.
missive
mission, missionary, commission, admission, permission, etc.
Mississippi
Missouri

(The last two words come from Indian names; the first few are from the Latin root *missus*, to send, hence the double *s*.)

Your problems will arise only in the forms of the six crucial words which contain a root beginning with *s* and which add the negative prefix *mis-*.

misspell _____	misspent _____
misstate _____	misspeak _____
misstep _____	misshapen _____

Understand the reason for the double *s* in these words, imprint their correct patterns on your visual memory, adjust to them kinesthetically—and the problem of whether to write *mis-* or *miss-* is one you will be able to solve without doubt or hesitation.

Now with *dis-* or *-diss*, on the other hand, we have a somewhat different problem.

There is a tendency, I have said, to use *mis-* where *miss-* is required.

Contrarily, there is an equally strong tendency to substitute an incorrect *diss-* for the required *dis-*.

Here again, confusion can be quickly and permanently eliminated by a clear understanding of basic principles—

And accurate, automatic reactions can be established through visual and kinesthetic training.

Like *mis-*, *dis-* is a prefix that attaches to a root form—

And, as in the case of *mis-* or *miss-*, the number of *s*'s is determined by whether or not the root itself starts with the letter *s*.

If the root starts with *s*, the complete word will contain a double *s*.

For example:

   dis- + *s*atisfy = di**ss**atisfy _____

   dis- + *s*imilar = di**ss**imilar _____

   dis- + *s*ervice = di**ss**ervice _____

But if the root does *not* start with *s*, the complete word will *not* contain a double *s*.
For example:

   dis- + **app**ear = dis**app**ear _____

   dis- + **app**oint = dis**app**oint _____

   dis- + **app**rove = dis**app**rove _____

   dis- + connect = disconnect _____

   dis- + agree = di**s**agree _____

Now let us explore these two points thoroughly.

Eliminating obscure words that appear only in the un-abridged dictionary, and which you would probably have no occasion to write, there are exactly nineteen different words, no more, that start with *diss-*. All others (and there are over twelve columns of such words in the dictionaries) start with *dis-*.

There is no need to memorize these nineteen *diss-* words, but if you completely understand how each one of them is engineered on the principle of a combination of the prefix *dis-* plus a root starting with *s* you can eliminate all possible confusion between these nineteen *diss-* words and the two-hundred odd *dis-* words.

Let us examine the nineteen forms one by one, noting in each case how the root starts with *s*.

1. DI**SS**ATISFY _____
The root is **S**ATISFY, the prefix has a negative force. Other forms, such as *dissatisfied, dissatisfaction, dissatisfactory*, etc., are of the same pattern.

2. DISSECT _____
-**S**ECT is the Latin root *to cut*; the prefix *DIS-* in this instance means *apart*; hence DI**S**SECT is to cut apart. (Similarly *bisect* is to cut in two, *trisect*, cut in three; *intersect*, cut between, etc.)

3. DISSEMBLE _____

The root is -SEMBLE, to appear, and is found in *semblance, resemble*, etc. *DIS-* again has a negative force, so that DISSEMBLE means to pretend, to disguise, in other words to appear other than in actuality.

4. DISSEMINATE _____

-SEMINATE comes from a Latin root *semen*, seed; the prefix *DIS-* means *in every direction*. So DISSEMI-NATE, by derivation, signifies *to scatter seeds in every direction* or *to scatter ideas widely*. A *seminary*, from the same root, is a place where seeds of knowledge are planted in the minds of students.

5. DISSENT _____

-SENT is a root meaning *to feel* or *think*, from which also derive *sentiment, sensation, sensual, sensible*, etc. *DIS-* in this case means *differently*, so to DISSENT is *to feel differently*, hence *disagree*. The noun DISSENSION follows the same pattern.

6. DISSERTATION _____

From -SERERE, to join. A DISSERTATION is a join-ing of words to discuss a subject apart (*DIS-*) from other subjects. The same root -*serere* also is found in *assert*.

7. DISSERVICE _____

Obviously SERVICE plus the negative *DIS-*.

8. DISSEVER _____

SEVER means *to separate*; to DISSEVER is *to sepa-rate apart*.

9. DISSIDENT _____

The root -SID is related to the SEDERE, *to sit,* which you will recall from *supersede*. A DISSIDENT sits apart from the rest of the group, in a manner of speaking.

10. DISSIMILAR _____

SIMILAR plus *DIS-*.

11. DISSIMULATE _____

This word has the same root as SIMILAR, Latin *simil*, like: to DISSIMULATE is to *disguise*, or *make unlike*.

12. DISSIPATE _____

This is one of the ten most frequently misspelled words in the language. The root is -SIP, to throw, plus *DIS-*, in every direction. So, when you DISSIPATE, you scatter your resources in every direction, often by sensual indulgence. This word has three danger spots—the double *s*, the following *i*, and the single *p*; and the understanding of the architecture of the word (DIS + SIP, to throw) takes care of all three simultaneously.

13. DISSOCIATE _____

DIS- plus ASSOCIATE, with the first two letters omitted from the root, so actually *DIS-* plus -SOCIATE.

14. DISSOLVE _____

DIS- plus the Latin root -SOLV, to loosen.

15. DISSOLUBLE _____

The adjective form of DISSOLVE has, strangely enough, the same meaning as SOLUBLE, the root to which *DIS-* is added.

16. DISSOLUTE _____

Formed by adding *DIS-* to another spelling of Latin SOLV-, to loosen. A DISSOLUTE character is morally loose, evil, wicked. The noun DISSOLUTION means a loosening up of all connections, so that everything falls apart, as in *the dissolution of the industrial empire*.

17. DISSONANCE _____

DIS-, differently, plus SONARE, to sound. DISSONANCE, then, is a combination of inharmonious sounds. *Resonant, unison, consonant,* and *sonorous* are all built on the same root, *sonare,* to sound.

18. DISSUADE _____

The root found in *persuade* (*-suadere,* to urge) plus *DIS-*, against.

19. DISSYLLABLE _____

This is the word SYLLABLE plus *DIS-*, two—hence a word of two syllables.

You can now combine your knowledge of the architecture of these nineteen words with visual memory to be able to recall, instantly, whether a *dis-* word belongs among the nineteen (and hence starts with *diss-*) or among the two hundred (and hence starts with *dis-*).

For further practice, examine the following chart. Make no attempt to memorize the nineteen *diss-* words. Instead, take three simple steps:

1. Understand how each *diss-* word is built—

2. Let the proper appearance register sharply on your visual memory—

3. Make a kinesthetic adjustment by writing each word in the space provided.

1. (DIS SATISFY)   dissatisfy _____
2. (DIS SECT, cut)   dissect _____
3. (DIS SEMBLE, seem)   dissemble _____
4. (DIS SEMEN, seed)   disseminate _____
5. (DIS SENT, feel)   dissent _____
6. (DIS SERERE, join words) dissertation _____
7. (DIS SERVICE)   disservice _____
8. (DIS SEVER, separate)   dissever _____
9. (DIS SID, sit)   dissident _____
10. (DIS SIMILAR)   dissimilar _____
11. (DIS SIMIL, like)   dissimulate _____
12. (DIS SIP, throw)   dissipate _____
13. (DIS SOCIATE)   dissociate _____
14. (DIS SOLV, loosen)   dissoluble _____
15. (DIS SOLV, loosen)   dissolve _____
16. (DIS SOLV, loosen)   dissolute _____
17. (DIS SONARE, sound)   dissonance _____
18. (DIS SUADERE, urge)   dissuade _____
19. (DIS SYLLABLE)   dissyllable _____

Once you have taken these three steps, you may be assured of one thing: You will never again be confused about whether to write *dis-* or *diss-* at the beginning of a word. And if you think you might wonder whether to use *dys-*, be assured on that count also: Only two common words start with *dys-*.

dysentery _____

dyspeptic _____

So let us now review the basic principles under which we have been operating.

Point 8

If a root starts with *s*, the addition of the prefix *mis-* or *dis-* will result in a double *s*—MISSPELLING, MISSTEP, DISSECT, DISSIPATE, etc.

Point 9

But if a root does not start with *s*, the addition of the prefix *mis-* or *dis-* will result in only a single *s*—MISAPPREHENSION, MISAPPLY, DISAPPEAR, DISAPPOINT, etc.

TEST YOURSELF

I. Attach the prefix *mis-* to the following roots, rewriting the complete words in the spaces provided.

1. spelling _____ (misspelling)
2. statement _____ (misstatement)
3. step _____ (misstep)
4. spent _____ (misspent)
5. shapen _____ (misshapen)
6. spoken _____ (misspoken)
7. hap _____ (mishap)
8. apprehend _____ (misapprehend)
9. construe _____ (misconstrue)

II. Attach the prefix *dis-* to the following roots, rewriting the complete words in the spaces provided.

1. appear _____ (disappear)
2. section _____ (dissection)
3. appoint _____ (disappoint)
4. -sent _____ (dissent)
5. approve _____ (disapprove)

6. -sertation _____ (dissertation)
7. agree _____ (disagree)
8. -sever _____ (dissever)
9. allow _____ (disallow)
10. -sidence _____ (dissidence)
11. appearance _____ (dis**app**earance)
12. service _____ (disservice)
13. -aster _____ (disaster)
14. -semble _____ (dissemble)
15. reputable _____ (disreputable)
16. similarity _____ (dissimilarity)
17. -sipate _____ (dissipate)
18. solve _____ (dissolve)
19. pleasure _____ (displeasure)
20. -seminate _____ (disseminate)
21. satisfy _____ (dissatisfy)
22. simulate _____ (dissimulate)
23. integrate _____ (disintegrate)
24. soluble _____ (dissoluble)
25. embark _____ (disembark)
26. -solute _____ (dissolute)
27. credit _____ (discredit)
28. like _____ (dislike)
29. -sonance _____ (dissonance)
30. syllable _____ (dissyllable)
31. connect _____ (disconnect)
32. entangle _____ (disentangle)
33. -sociate _____ (dissociate)
34. -suade _____ (dissuade)
35. comfort _____ (discomfort)

PRETEST

1. persist**ant** *or* persist**ent**?
2. insist**ant** *or* insist**ent**?
3. depend**ant** *or* depend**ent**?
4. emba**r**assed *or* emba**rr**assed?
5. a**n**oint *or* a**nn**oint?

MNEMONICS

A mnemonic, as you know, highlights the "danger spot" of a word.

It ties up, by some meaningful association, the "area of error," the place where most people go wrong, with some easily spelled word or with some logically connected phrases or ideas, in such a way that the correct pattern of a difficult word is immediately clear.

You will recall that:

—in *occurrence*, the crucial letters are *-rre*, and the mnemonic *current event* helps avoid any possibility of error.

—in *superintendent*, the mnemonic *rent* highlights the correct ending.

—in *inoculate*, the mnemonic *inject* focuses attention on the single *n* and single *c*.

—in *dependable* and *indispensable*, the mnemonic *able worker* indicates the proper spelling of the final syllable, *-able*.

The words on which you have tested yourself in this chapter also lend themselves to quick learning through clear-cut, easily recalled mnemonics.

1. (persist**ant** *or* persist**ent**?)
2. (insist**ant** *or* insist**ent**?)
3. (depend**ant** *or* depend**ent**?)

-Ant or *-ent*? This is a question that causes considerable confusion and unhappiness, a question that constantly plagues the inefficient speller. Unfortunately there are no broad rules, no sweeping generalizations that can immediately separate the sheep from the goats, no way of keeping the *-ant* words from getting mixed up with the *-ent* words.[1]

Four words are among those that cause particular trouble: superintend**ent**, persist**ent**, insist**ent** and depend**ent**—and one mnemonic covers all four.

You recall that the superintend**ent** of an apartm**ent** house collects the r**ent**. He is generally persist**ent** and insist**ent** about it and his job is often depend**ent** on his success. Now these statements may or may not constitute sound psychology, economics, or sociology—no matter. Some mnemonics, as you will shortly discover, can be weird to an outrageous degree, but if there is some relationship in meaning and spelling between a mnemonic and a problem word, truth and soundness and sanity are of secondary importance.

So simply get a picture in your mind of a superintend**ent** collecting r**ent** being persist**ent** and insist**ent**, and feeling that his job is depend**ent** on his collections, and you have permanently mastered four words that are frequently misspelled.

---

[1]Chapter 26 will explore the problem of *-ant, -ent, -ance, -ence* in all its aspects and will explain why visual training is the most efficient solution.

Needless to say, all forms of these words follow a similar pattern:

superintend**ence** _____   depend**ence** _____
persist**ence** _____   depend**ency** _____
insist**ence** _____   independ**ence** _____

And notice the contrast between depend**able**, undepend**able** and depend**ent**, independ**ent**. With the letter *a* preceding *-ble*, you might not expect a sudden change of vowel before *-nt*. Remember, however, that the unexpected is highly normal in English spelling.

     Correct Spellings: persist**ent** _____
                         insist**ent** _____
                         depend**ent** _____
     Mnemonic: **rent**

4. (emba**r**assed *or* emba**rr**assed?)

Here the crucial question is the number of *r*'s and *s*'s. Most people misspell the word by using only one *r*, but every possible combination can occasionally be found. Consider this sentence: "**Two r**obbers were emba**rr**assed when they were sent to **S**ing **S**ing [a New York State penitentiary]."

Two robbers—two *r*'s
Sing **S**ing—two *s*'s

For a small percentage of spellers, the third syllable of *embarrassed* is a second area of difficulty—there is a temptation to suit the spelling to the sound and write *-ess*. If you are similarly tempted, think of this sentence: "When you're emba**rrass**ed, you feel like an **ass**."

All forms of this word follow the same pattern.

emba**rrass**ment _____   emba**rr**asses _____
emba**rr**assing _____   emba**rr**ass _____

     Correct Spelling: emba**rr**assed _____
     Mnemonics: **Two r**obbers emba**rr**assed in **S**ing **S**ing; feel like an **ass.**

5. (an**o**int *or* a**nn**oint?)

The important letter in *anoint* is the single *n* following the *a*. (Whenever the word is misspelled, as it often is, a double *n* is erroneously used.) When someone is an**o**inted, a**n o**il is generally used.
So:

a**n o**il—an**o**int

(As you go on with your study of words you will begin to group those of similar difficulty. *Anoint* with one *n* will remind you of *inoculate* with one *n*.)

MNEMONICS CHART

Correct Pattern	*Mnemonic*
persist**ent** _____	**rent**
insist**ent** _____	**rent**
depend**ent** _____	**rent**
emba**rr**assed _____	**two** robbers in **S**ing **S**ing; *ass*
an**o**int _____	a**n o**il

A Footnote on Embarrassment

The suffix *-ment* is added to a verb to form a noun. It is usually added to the verb as is, with no additions. For example, *embezzlement, encouragement, entanglement, advertisement,* etc. As you see, many verbs end in the letter *e,* and so *-ement* is a common and reputable ending.

But *embarrass* does not end in *e,* so there is no *e* after the *-ss* of *embarrassment.* (The incorrect pattern, *embarrassement,* is frequently found in unsophisticated writing.) *Embarrassment* belongs in the same class as *accomplishment, bewilderment, enlightenment,* etc.—no *e* at the end of the verb, no *e* preceding the *-ment.*

So watch your step on *embarrass* and its various forms—there are more temptations to go wrong than confront a newly landed sailor with all his back pay in his pocket.

TEST YOURSELF

I. Check the correct pattern.
1. (a) persistant,   (b) persistent   (b)
2. (a) insistant,   (b) insistent   (b)
3. (a) dependant,   (b) dependent   (b)
4. (a) embarassed,   (b) embarrassed   (b)
5. (a) anoint,   (b) annoint   (a)

II. Recall the mnemonic for each word.
1. occu**rre**nce ＿＿＿＿ (**curre**nt event)
2. superintend**ent** ＿＿＿＿ (**rent**)
3. **in**oculate ＿＿＿＿ (**inject**)
4. indispens**able** ＿＿＿＿ (**able** worker)
5. depend**able** ＿＿＿＿ (**able** worker)
6. s**ie**ge ＿＿＿＿ (c**i**ty)
7. s**ei**ze ＿＿＿＿ (n**e**ck)
8. ba**tt**alion ＿＿＿＿ (ba**tt**le)
9. para**ll**el ＿＿＿＿ (**all** tracks)
10. fri**ca**ssee ＿＿＿＿ (**ca**sserole)
11. persist**ent** ＿＿＿＿ (**rent**)
12. insist**ent** ＿＿＿＿ (**rent**)
13. depend**ent** ＿＿＿＿ (**rent**)
14. emba**rr**a**ss**ed ＿＿＿＿ (**two r**obbers,
                       Sing Sing, **ass**)
15. a**n**o**i**nt ＿＿＿＿ (**an oi**l)

III. Decide on the missing letter or letters, then rewrite
the complete word.
1. persist—nt ＿＿＿＿ (e)
2. insist—nt ＿＿＿＿ (e)
3. depend—nt ＿＿＿＿ (e)
4. emba—ed ＿＿＿＿ (rrass)
5. a—oint ＿＿＿＿ (n)
6. persist—nce ＿＿＿＿ (e)
7. insist—nce ＿＿＿＿ (e)
8. depend—nce ＿＿＿＿ (e)

9. depend—ncy _____ (e)
10. independ—nce _____ (e)
11. superintend—nce _____ (e)
12. emba—ment _____ (rrass)
13. a—ointed _____ (n)
14. emba—ing _____ (rrass)
15. occu—nce _____ (rre)

8

How to Decide Between *ie* and *ei* in Long Syllables

PROBLEMS

receive *or* recieve?
niece *or* neice?
inviegle *or* inveigle?
seize *or* sieze?

SOLUTION

You have no doubt heard of the ingenious veteran of many a spelling battle. Despairing of ever straightening himself out on whether to use *ei* or *ie*, he evolved a plan which was practically foolproof. When he had to write a word like *receive* (or *recieve*?), *believe* (or *beleive*?), *achieve* (or *acheive*?), etc., he would make the *e* and *i* look identical, and place the dot squarely between them, as follows:

recieve
believe
achieve

That is admittedly as good a way as any to cover up one's ignorance and avoid getting into trouble. But, actually, to learn, once and for all, when to write *ie* and when to write *ei* is so simple that it is unnecessary to descend to subterfuge, however successful.

There is, for example, the mnemonic rhyme that every schoolchild knows:

> I before E
> Except after C
> Or when sounded like A
> As in *neighbor* or *weigh*.

This is a good, reliable principle, provided you are aware of the possibility of exceptional cases.

Of the hundred or more English words which contain the combination *ie* or *ei* with the sound of *long-E-as-in-grief*, all but seventeen are covered by the *first two lines* of the jingle; and those pronounced with *long-A-as-in-weigh* are completely covered by the *last two lines* of the jingle.

But let's not go too fast.

We know that if the sound of the combination is *long-E-as-in-grief*, the proper pattern is *ie* after any letter *except c.*

For instance:

believe _____	relieve _____
grieve _____	piece _____
achieve _____	priest _____
fiend _____	brief _____
field _____	shriek _____
yield _____	grief _____
siege _____	thief _____
pier _____	cashier _____
pierce _____	rabies _____
niece _____	frontier _____

And we know that if the immediately preceding letter is *c*, the correct combination is *ei*.

For instance:

receive _____	conceive _____
receipt _____	conceit _____
ceiling _____	preconceive _____
deceive _____	perceive _____
deceit _____	etc.

This is so simple, we need spend no further time on it: generally *ie*, but after the letter *c, ei*. (Remember, however, that we are considering only those words in which the *ie* or *ei* combination has the sound of *long-E-as-in grief*.)

I have said that all but seventeen words with the sound of *long-E-as-in-grief* are covered by the first two lines of the traditional jingle.

What about the seventeen nonconformists?

These seventeen present no insuperable problem.

One of them is in a class by itself. Despite the immediately preceding *c*, the *ie* combination is used. This lone and unique rebel is:

1. financier _____

Seven others are most important. *Although there is no immediately preceding c, the ei combination is nevertheless used.* These words merit study; they are often misspelled.

2. seize _____	6. weird _____
3. seizure _____	7. weir (a river dam) __
4. leisure _____	8. inveigle (Pronounced
5. sheik _____	either *in-VEE-g'l* or
	in-VAY-g'l)
	_____

Two others belong with the preceding seven, but are rarely misspelled:

9. either _____ 10. neither _____

Three more are terms from chemistry:

11. cod**ei**ne[1] _____   13. caff**ei**ne[1] _____
12. prot**ei**n[1] _____

And the last four are proper names:

14. K**ei**th _____   16. N**ei**l _____
15. R**ei**d _____   17. O'N**ei**ll _____

Of these seventeen, then, seven require special study—these cause the most confusion:

s**ei**ze _____   l**ei**sure _____
s**ei**zure _____   w**ei**rd _____
sh**ei**k _____   w**ei**r _____
inv**ei**gle _____

Commit these seven to visual memory, be aware of the other ten exceptional cases, and keep in mind that otherwise the jingle operates. You have then mastered *ie-ei* combinations in all words with the sound of *long-E-as-in-grief*.

To recapitulate the basic principle under which the words of this chapter have thus far operated, let us formulate:

Point 10

In words with the sound of *long-E-as-in-grief*, *ie* is the general combination, with *ei* the required pattern directly after the letter *c*—in all but seventeen special cases.

And now let us consider the last two lines of the jingle:

>Or when sounded like A
>As in *neighbor* or *weigh*.

This part of the mnemonic is 100 per cent trustworthy—if the sound of the combination is *long-A-as-in-neighbor-or-weigh*, the pattern is always *ei*.

For example:

---

[1]Popular pronunciation gives each of these words a two-syllable pronunciation, with the long *e* sound in the second syllable. Many dictionaries, however, suggest a rarely heard three-syllable pronunciation.

neigh _____	skein _____
weigh _____	chow mein _____
weight _____	vein _____
freight _____	inveigh _____
rein _____	inveigle _____
	(pronounced *in-VAY-g'l*
reign _____	or *in-VEE-g'l*)
veil _____	heinous _____
	(pronounced *HAY*-nus)

However, the jingle does not go quite far enough; *ei* is also the correct combination for the sound of *long-I-as-in-height*.

For example:

height _____	Fahrenheit _____
sleight _____	kaleidoscope _____
(of hand)	
	seismic _____
gneiss _____	(pronounced *SIZE-mic*)
(a form of rock;	
pronounced *NICE*)	seismograph _____
stein _____	leitmotif _____
(of beer)	(a musical term;
	pronounced *LYTE-mo-teef*)

There are, as it happens, three important exceptions to the principle that the sound of *long-I-as-in-height* is spelled *ei* rather than *ie*. These special cases, rarely misspelled, are:

fiery _____	hierarchy _____
hieroglyphic _____	_____

So we also operate under the following basic principle:

Point 11

In words with the sound of *long-A-as-in-neighbor* or

long-I-as-in-height, *ei* is the correct combination in all but three special cases—*fiery, hieroglyphic, hierarchy*.

Your decision between *ie* and *ei* in long syllables is governed, then, by five simple rules—

1. For *long-E-as-in-grief*, use *ie* generally.
2. Change to *ei* directly after the letter *c*.
3. For *long-A-as-in-weigh*, use *ei* at all times.
4. For *long-I-as-in-height*, use *ei* except in *fiery, hieroglyphic* and *hierarchy*.
5. Keep in mind seventeen special exceptions to rules 1 and 2, seven of which are particularly important.

TEST YOURSELF

Decide on the proper combination, *ie* or *ei*, then rewrite the complete word.

1. f—rce _____ (ie)
2. bel—ve _____ (ie)
3. n—ce _____ (ie)
4. rec—ve _____ (ei)
5. c—ling _____ (ei)
6. f—ld _____ (ie)
7. ach—ve _____ (ie)
8. cod—ne _____ (ei)
9. p—ce _____ (ie)
10. financ—r _____ (ie)
11. y—ld _____ (ie)
12. f—nd _____ (ie)
13. conc—ve _____ (ei)
14. p—rce _____ (ie)
15. shr—k _____ (ie)
16. repr—ve _____ (ie)
17. prot—n _____ (ei)
18. br—f _____ (ie)
19. s—ze _____ (ei)
20. l—f _____ (ie)

21. m—n _____ (ie)
22. s—zure _____ (ei)
23. retr—ve _____ (ie)
24. w—rd _____ (ei)
25. sh—ld _____ (ie)
26. sh—k _____ (ei)
27. l—sure _____ (ei)
28. rel—f _____ (ie)
29. w—r _____ (ei)
30. cash—r _____ (ie)
31. dec—ve _____ (ei)
32. chiffon—r _____ (ie)
33. dec—t _____ (ei)
34. R—d _____ (ei)
35. front—r _____ (ie)
36. f—rcely _____ (ie)
37. —ther _____ (ei)
38. pr—st _____ (ie)
39. rab—s _____ (ie)
40. N—l _____ (ei)
41. scab—s _____ (ie)
42. caff—ne _____ (ei)
43. chandel—r _____ (ie)
44. K—th _____ (ei)
45. rec—pt _____ (ei)
46. inv—gle _____ (ei)
47. w—ght _____ (ei)
48. r—gn _____ (ei)
49. h—nous _____ (ei)
50. v—n _____ (ei)
51. f—ry _____ (ie)
52. sl—ght _____ (ei)
53. sk—n _____ (ei)
54. —derdown _____ (ei)

55. s—smic _____ (ei)
56. h—roglyphic _____ (ie)
57. h—ght _____ (ei)
58. kal—doscope _____ (ei)

A Footnote on the Pronunciation of Inveigle

There is, as you probably know, a numerous class of English words which have two current pronunciations. There is the popular, everyday form used by the average man or woman. And there is also the supposedly "cultivated" form, which has a great attraction for some people who like to consider themselves linguistically sophisticated.

Cases in point are *exquisite, coupon, adult, duty,* and *gratis.* Common, and fully acceptable, pronunciations for these words are *ex-KWIZ-it, KYOO-pon, AD-ult, DOO-tee,* and *GRAT-is;* but there are those speakers who prefer the more scholarly *EX-kwi-zit, KOO-pon, a-DULT, DYOO-tee,* and *GRAY-tis.* And a further case in point is *inveigle.* The scholarly, conservative pronunciation is *in-VEE-g'l,* which throws the word into the exceptional group of those that have a *long-E-as-in-grief* syllable, but which, like *leisure, weird, seize,* etc., nevertheless contains the spelling pattern *ei* not preceded by *c.*

However, for years, the very, very popular pronunciation of *inveigle* has been *in-VAY-g'l,* and is so sanctioned (along with *in-VEE-g'l*) by up-to-date dictionaries. As *in-VAY-g'l,* the word is no spelling problem—it belongs with all those which contain a *long-A-as-in-weigh* syllable and are spelled *ei.*

So pronounce *inveigle* however it sounds most comfortable to you—but spell it only *inveigle.*

9

9   *(Fourth Day, continued)*

How to Decide Between
ie and *ei*
in Short Syllables

PROBLEMS

si**e**ve *or* se**i**ve?
fre**i**nd *or* fri**e**nd?
misch**ie**f *or* misch**ei**f?

SOLUTION

You will recall that the problem of *ie* or *ei* in long
syllables is solved under the following rules:

1. *Long-E-as-in-grief*, use *ie*:
   achi**e**ve _____   thi**e**f _____
   ni**e**ce _____   si**e**ge _____

2. Exceptions to remember are:
   s**ei**ze _____   l**ei**sure _____
   s**ei**zure _____   sh**ei**k _____
   w**ei**rd _____   inv**ei**gle _____
   w**ei**r _____

3. After *c*, use *ei*:
   re**cei**ve _____   **cei**ling _____
   The notable exception is
         finan**cie**r _____

4. *Long-A-as-in-neighbor*, use *ei*:

freight _____   weight _____

rein _____   vein _____

5. *Long-I-as-in-height*, use *ei*:

sleight _____   seismic _____

stein _____   Fahrenheit _____

6. Exceptions are:

hierarchy _____   fiery _____

hieroglyphic _____

All right—so far, so good.

But what if an *ie-ei* combination has a pronunciation other than long *E*, long *A*, or long *I*?

What if the combination has a *short* sound, as in *forfeit* (short *I*), or as in *friend* (short *E*)?

Then we have to be careful.

For in special instances we use *ei*.

But in other instances we use *ie*.

This may at first sound confusing, so let's go slow.

Item: For short syllables, we use *ei* in the *-feit* words:

counterfeit _____   surfeit _____

forfeit _____

Item: ei also in the *-eign* words:

foreign _____   sovereign _____

foreigner _____   sovereignty _____

Item: And *ei* again in these two words:

nonpareil _____   heifer _____
  (pronounced *non-pa-RELL*)

Become visually and kinesthetically adjusted to the combination *ei* in *nonpareil*, in *heifer*, and in the *-eit* and *-eign* words—and the problem of *ie* or *ei* in short syllables can be solved instantaneously and automatically—

For all others, without exception, are spelled *ie*.

For example:

handkerchief _____	ancient _____
kerchief _____	efficient _____
mischief _____	omniscience _____
mischievous _____	conscience _____
efficient _____	quotient _____
deficient _____	transient _____
sufficient _____	sieve _____
proficient _____	friend _____
patient _____	etc.

Nothing, I think you'll agree, can be less confusing. The basic principle is perfectly clear:

Point 12

In short syllables, the general combination is *ie*. However, in *nonpareil* and *heifer*, and in *-eit* and *-eign* words, the correct pattern is *ei*.

TEST YOURSELF

Decide on the missing combination (*ie* or *ei*), then rewrite the complete word.

1. forf—t _____ (ei)
2. for—gn _____ (ei)
3. counterf—t _____ (ei)
4. sover—gn _____ (ei)
5. surf—t _____ (ei)
6. s—ve _____ (ie)
7. handkerch—f _____ (ie)
8. nonpar—l _____ (ei)
9. misch—vous _____ (ie)
10. anc—nt _____ (ie)
11. h—fer _____ (ei)
12. kerch—f _____ (ie)
13. fr—nd _____ (ie)
14. trans—nt _____ (ie)

A Footnote on Nonpareil and Friend

Students of the French language have no difficulty spelling *nonpareil*—this word is a direct import from the Gallic tongue and, as so often happens, retains its foreign spelling even though the pronunciation has been completely Anglicized. (We say *non-pa-RELL*, quite different from what the French say.)

Pareil is the French term for *equal; non* is of course a sign of the negative. So in French, as also in English, the word means *having no equal, in a class by itself.* It is not in particularly common use, except, as it happens, as the name of a type of candy with a chocolate bottom and little white sugar dots. And there is no reason why you should have to be able to spell it, unless you have a passion for feeling completely self-assured that you know the correct pattern of any word that has even the remotest chance of being offered you; or unless, of course, you are preparing for the spelling section of a Civil Service test, on which the most amazing words always occur.

Friend, however, is in a very different category—it is a most common word in everyday use, and anyone beyond the fourth grade of grammar school is expected to be able to spell it correctly. Yet, for some strange and unexplainable reason, many otherwise educated people are stumped by this simple word, never quite sure whether to write *ie* or *ei*—and often, unhappily, finally deciding on *ei*. If the word was ever a problem to you, it need no longer be so; you know that short syllables are usually spelled *ie* except in the *-eign* and *-eit* groups and in the two special words *heifer* and *nonpareil*.

10

First Review

Let us stop for a moment, now, so you can catch your breath.

Let us review all you've learned thus far.

Let us wrap all the facts and figures into a neat package.

We have thoroughly covered the following basic principles:

Supersede is the only word in the English language ending in *-sede*.

super**sede** _____

Three, and only three, words end in *-ceed*, keyed to the phrase *Full Speed Ahead*.

suc**ceed** _____   ex**ceed** _____
pro**ceed** _____

All other "seed" words end in *-cede*.

ac**cede** _____   pre**cede** _____
se**cede** _____   re**cede** _____
etc.

Procedure and *procedural*, forms of one of the three "speed" words, do not contain a double *e*.

procedure _____   proce**d**ural _____

Most words end in *-ize* in preference to *-ise* or *-yze*.

apolog**ize** _____ hypnot**ize** _____
etc.

Two common words end in *-yze*.

anal**yze** _____ paral**yze** _____

Thirty-six common words end in *-ise*.

adv**ise** _____ surpr**ise** _____
dev**ise** _____ surm**ise** _____
etc.

Miss- occurs at the begining of a word if the root starts with *s*.

misshapen _____ **miss**pelling _____
etc.

Diss- occurs at the beginning of a word if the root starts with *s*.

dissatisfy _____ **diss**imilar _____
etc.

Dis- occurs at the beginning of a word if the root does not start with *s*.

disappear _____ **dis**approve _____
disappoint _____ **dis**concert _____
etc.

Dys- occurs at the beginning of two words:

dyspeptic _____ **dys**entery _____

For the long *E* sound, *ie* is the usual combination:

n**ie**ce _____ f**ie**ld _____
ach**ie**ve _____ p**ie**ce _____
etc.

Seven important words are exceptions to the *ie* rule:

seize _____   weird _____
seizure _____   weir _____
leisure _____   inveigle _____
sheik _____

However, directly after the letter *c*, *ei* is used.

receive _____   ceiling _____

With one glaring exception:

finan**cier** _____

In syllables with a *long A* pronunciation, *ei* is required.

n**ei**gh _____   v**ei**l _____

In syllables with a *long I* pronunciation, *ei* is again required.

h**ei**ght _____   st**ei**n _____

Three exceptions are:

fi**e**ry _____   hi**e**rarchy _____
hi**e**roglyphic _____

In syllables with a *short* pronunciation, *ei* is required in the *-eit* and *-eign* words:

counterf**ei**t _____   for**ei**gn _____
                etc.

And also in two special words:

nonpar**ei**l _____   h**ei**fer _____

For all other words with *short* syllables *ie* is correct.

s**ie**ve _____   anc**ie**nt _____
fr**ie**nd _____   consc**ie**nce _____
                etc.

FIRST REVIEW TEST

I. Check the correct pattern.
1. (a) supercede, (b) supersede   (b)
2. (a) procede,   (b) proceed   (b)
3. (a) excede,   (b) exceed   (b)
4. (a) precede,   (b) preceed   (a)
5. (a) conceed,   (b) concede   (b)
6. (a) procedure, (b) proceedure   (a)

II. Attach the correct ending, choosing between *-ise*, *-ize*, and *-yze*, rewriting the complete word.
1. paral— _____ (yze)
2. anal— _____ (yze)
3. advert— _____ (ise)
4. appr— _____ (ise)
5. surm— _____ (ise)
6. superv— _____ (ise)
7. improv— _____ (ise)
8. comprom— _____ (ise)
9. surpr— _____ (ise)
10. compr— _____ (ise)
11. apolog— _____ (ize)
12. character— _____ (ize)
13. memor— _____ (ize)
14. ostrac— _____ (ize)

III. Begin each word with *mis-* or *miss-*, as required, rewriting the complete word.
1. —pelling _____ (miss)
2. —tatement _____ (miss)
3. —tep _____ (miss)
4. —pent _____ (miss)
5. —construe _____ (mis)
6. —hap _____ (mis)
7. —hapen _____ (miss)
8. —cellaneous _____ (mis)

79

IV. Begin each word with *dis-*, *diss-*, or *dys-*, as required, rewriting the complete word.

1. —appear _____ (dis)
2. —appoint _____ (dis)
3. —approve _____ (dis)
4. —peptic _____ (dys)
5. —entery _____ (dys)
6. —atisfy _____ (diss)
7. —ertation _____ (diss)
8. —ever _____ (diss)
9. —imilar _____ (diss)
10. —ociate _____ (diss)
11. —olute _____ (diss)
12. —uade _____ (diss)
13. —yllable _____ (diss)
14. —agree _____ (dis)
15. —allow _____ (dis)

V. Fill in *ie* or *ei*, as required, rewriting the complete word.

1. rec—ve _____ (ei)
2. dec—t _____ (ei)
3. bel—ve _____ (ie)
4. f—ld _____ (ie)
5. n—ce _____ (ie)
6. y—ld _____ (ie)
7. s—zure _____ (ei)
8. financ—r _____ (ie)
9. sh—k _____ (ei)
10. w—rd _____ (ei)
11. w—r _____ (ei)
12. l—sure _____ (ei)
13. chandel—r _____ (ie)
14. w—gh _____ (ei)
15. h—nous _____ (ei)
16. inv—gle _____ (ei)
17. r—gn _____ (ei)

18. inv—gh _____ (ei)
19. h—ght _____ (ei)
20. st—n _____ (ei)
21. f—ry _____ (ie)
22. counterf—t _____ (ei)
23. forf—t _____ (ei)
24. sover—gn _____ (ei)
25. misch—f _____ (ie)
26. s—ve _____ (ie)
27. fr—nd _____ (ie)
28. consc—nce _____ (ie)

11

When to Drop a Final *e*

PROBLEMS

desireable *or* desirable?
stoney *or* stony?
likeable *or* likable?

SOLUTION

There is, then, a certain rudimentary logic to English spelling.

No one in his right mind would call our system of spelling "completely logical," "eminently logical," or even "fairly logical"; on the other hand, it is somewhat prejudiced to label it "thoroughly illogical" or "absolutely fantastic." There are some strong threads of logic running through it, with many illogical threads interspersed—and with a little practice and understanding it is possible, as I hope you have seen, to come to terms with spelling, to declare a kind of armed truce, even to arrive quite close to mastery.

One of your potent allies in the conquest and mastery of English spelling is a basic human ability—the ability to become used to something if it is repeated often enough.

Take, for example, the word *come*. It would be far more logical to spell it *cum* or even *kum*, but no normal human being who has progressed beyond the fourth grade in school is ever tempted to spell it in that sane and sensible way. (How sensible *cum* would be may be judged from the fact that *come* is derived from the Anglo-Saxon word *cuman*.) Indeed, *cum* or *kum* appearing in a page of print would at once arrest the eye. Sane and sensible as it may be, it looks ridiculous—because, through repetition and habit, we are completely adjusted to seeing and writing *come*.

Similarly, no one ever misspells *move, like, love, prove, hate, make, wave, give, change, desire*, etc. In each case we use the final *e*, expect to see it in print, and require it to pronounce the word correctly.

But some of us become overly attached to that final *-e*, and through either accident or ignorance keep it in a word even when it no longer belongs there. In the writing of a poor speller, it is not uncommon to find errors like:

comeing	moveing	likeing
loveable	proveable	hateing
makeing	waveing	giveing
changeing	arriveal	desireable
	etc.	

If every one of these spellings looks peculiar to you, this is not the type of error you make. And you can, with a little thought, see the basic principle that operates:

Point 13

When a word ends in *e*—

> (*prove, stone, value, desire*)

Drop that *e*—

> (*prov-, ston-, valu-, desir-*)

Before adding a suffix that begins with a vowel.

> (*prov-ing, ston-y,*[1] *valu-able, desir-able*, etc.)

---

[1] Many people think we have only five vowesl, *a,e,i,o,u*; but *y* is almost always a vowel if it is not the first letter of a word.

Nothing very unusual here—an important tendency in English is the avoidance of two vowels where one will do. So the following spellings are correct:

(come)	coming
(move)	moving, movable[2]
(like)	liking, likable[2]
(love)	loving, lovable[2]
(prove)	proving, provable
(hate)	hating
(make)	making
(value)	valuable
(wave)	waving
(give)	giving
(stone)	stony
(change)	changing
(sale)	salable
(bone)	bony
(desire)	desirable, desiring
(arrive)	arriving, arrival
(argue)	arguing, argued

So you know that it is normal and proper to drop a final *e* before adding a vowel ending.

What if you add a consonant ending, such as *-ment*, *-ful*, or *-ness*?

Point 14

Final *e* is *retained* when you add a suffix beginning with a consonant.

For example:

WORD	CONSONANT	VOWEL
state	stat**e**ment	stat/ing
refine	refin**e**ment	refin/ing
sure	sur**e**ness	sur/est

---

[2]*Likeable* and *loveable* are not wrong; but *likable* and *lovable* are the preferred spellings. *Moveable* is also acceptable, but *movable* is preferred.

grace	graceful	grac/ing
care	careful	car/ing
encourage	encouragement	encourag/ing
waste	wasteful	wast/ing
true	trueness	tru/er
vague	vaguely	vagu/er

And that's all there is to it—drop final *e* before a vowel, keep it before a consonant.

Such a simple principle, you probably suspect, is subject to exceptions.

What these exceptions are, and how they operate, we will consider in subsequent chapters.[3]

TEST YOURSELF

Rewrite each word, adding the indicated suffix.

1. like + *able* _____ (likable)
2. love + *able* _____ (lovable)
3. prove + *able* _____ (provable)
4. give + *ing* _____ (giving)
5. bone + *y* _____ (bony)
6. stone + *y* _____ (stony)
7. argue + *ing* _____ (arguing)
8. value + *able* _____ (valuable)
9. care + *ful* _____ (careful)
10. true + *ness* _____ (trueness)

[3]See Chapter 12, page 94, Chapter 14, page 102, and Chapter 15, page 113.

MNEMONICS
Four *(Sixth Day, continued)*

PRETEST

1. exhillarate, exhillerate, *or* exhilarate?
2. vicious *or* viscious?
3. rediculous *or* ridiculous?
4. description *or* discription?
5. repetition *or* repitition?
6. reccomend *or* recommend?
7. buisness *or* business?
8. holiday *or* holliday?
9. abscence *or* absence?
10. dispair *or* despair?

MNEMONICS

Understanding is a matter of seeing relationships.

As you begin to understand English spelling, you will see more and more relationships—between various words, between the letters of words, between the pattern of a word's spelling and the Latin or Greek root from which the word derives.

You are now beginning to understand the reasons behind the correct spellings of English words.

You know that the reason behind the ending in *supersede* is its Latin derivation, *sedeo*, to sit.

You know that the reason behind the endings in *accede, precede, secede*, etc., is their Latin derivation *cedo*, to go.

You know that the reason behind the double *s* in *misspelling, misshapen, dissyllable, dissuade*, etc., is that the prefix *mis-* or *dis-*, is attached to a root starting with an *s*.

You know that *dissipate* is spelled as it is because the prefix *dis-* is tacked on to the root *sip*, to throw.

You can now also begin to think of words in groups. *Superintendent, persistent, insistent*, and *dependent* belong in one group. *Anoint* and *inoculate* belong in another. *Succeed, proceed*, and *exceed* belong in a third. *Paralyze* and *analyze* belong in a fourth. *Dysentery* and *dyspeptic* belong in a fifth. And so on.

The sharpening of your sense of relationships will help you to build accurate and automatic habits of good spelling, will increase your confidence in your ability to choose the correct pattern under all circumstances.

Our interest in this chapter will again be focused on relationships, in this case the relationship between a difficult form of a word and an easily spelled form of the same word.

Let me illustrate.

1. HILARIOUS, *very merry, noisily gay*, is rarely misspelled even by the most confused and inefficient of spellers, for the pattern exactly follows the sound. Yet another form of the same word, EXHILARATE, is almost consistently misspelled by even the most literate and sophisticated of writers. If you think of the easily spelled HILARIOUS, and note the single *l* followed by *a*, you will have no difficulty spelling

EXHILARATE _____

2. VICE is the easily spelled form of VICIOUS—see this relationship and you'll feel no temptation to misspell the word.

VICIOUS _____

3. RIDICULE, spelled exactly as it sounds, rarely causes trouble; keep this form in mind when you write RIDICULOUS, which is not necessarily spelled exactly as it sounds—some speakers make the first syllable identical to that in *reading*.

RIDICULOUS _____

4. For some unexplainable reason, practically no one misspells DESCRIBE—but approximately 20 per cent of any random group of literate people misspell the noun form DESCRIPTION. Note the identical first syllable on both forms:

DESCRIPTION _____

5. REPEAT, like DESCRIBE, is practically never misspelled—but its related form, REPETITION, frequently is. Note that in REPEAT the *p* is followed by *e*—as also in REPETITION. (The same principle works in COMPETE —COMPETITION; an *e* after the *p* in each case.)

REPETITION _____

6. COMMEND is rarely misspelled—keep the word in mind when you add the prefix *re-*, *again*. So to COMMEND *again* is to

RECOMMEND _____

7. BUSY has never, to my knowledge, stumped a speller who has advanced beyond the third grade of elementary school—but its related form BUSINESS (BUSY + NESS) takes its toll of approximately 10 per cent of literate people.

BUSINESS _____

8. HOLIDAY has one *l*—it is a HOLY DAY (originally, holidays were all of religious significance), and the *y* changes to *i* as it does when BUSYNESS becomes BUSINESS.

HOLIDAY _____

9. The obviously related form AB**SE**NT has no *c*—hence AB**SE**NCE, not *abscence*.

AB**SE**NCE _____

10. D**E**SPAIR does not follow the pronunciation—but its allied form D**E**SPERATE does, at least in the first syllable; and from D**E**SPERATE we have the key to the first syllable *des*- rather than *dis*-.

D**E**SPERATE _____

MNEMONICS CHART

Note, then, what we are doing.

As a general mnemonic, we are taking a difficult-to-spell form of a word and relating it to an easily spelled form—and the easy form steers us away from any error in the pattern of the confusing form.

Correct Pattern	*Mnemonic*
1. exhilarate _____	hilarious
2. vicious _____	vice
3. ridiculous _____	ridicule
4. description _____	describe
5. repetition _____	repeat
6. recommend _____	commend
7. business _____	busy
8. holiday _____	holy
9. absence _____	absent
10. despair _____	desperate

TEST YOURSELF

I. Check the correct pattern.

1. (a) reccomend,	(b) recommend	(b)
2. (a) description,	(b) discription	(a)
3. (a) buisness,	(b) business	(b)
4. (a) holiday,	(b) holliday	(a)

5. (a) abscence,   (b) absence   (b)
6. (a) dispairing,   (b) despairing   (b)
7. (a) viscious,   (b) vicious   (b)
8. (a) exhillerate,   (b) exhillarate,   (c) exhilarate   (c)
9. (a) ridiculous,   (b) rediculous   (a)
10. (a) repetition,   (b) repitition   (a)

II. Recall the mnemonic for each word.

1. exhil**a**rate _____ (**hila**rious)
2. vi**ci**ous _____ (**vice**)
3. ri**di**culous _____ (**ridi**cule)
4. de**s**cription _____ (de**s**cribe)
5. rep**e**tition _____ (rep**ea**t)
6. re**comm**end _____ (**comm**end)
7. bu**si**ness _____ (**bu**sy)
8. abs**en**ce _____ (abs**en**t)
9. ho**li**day _____ (ho**ly**)
10. de**s**pair _____ (de**s**perate)
11. occu**rr**ence _____ (cu**rr**ent event)
12. superintend**ent** _____ (**rent**)
13. in**o**culate _____ (in**ject**)
14. indispens**able** _____ (**able** worker)
15. depend**able** _____ (**able** worker)
16. si**e**ge _____ (c**i**ty)
17. s**ei**ze _____ (neck)
18. ba**tt**alion _____ (ba**tt**le)
19. para**ll**el _____ (a**ll** tracks)
20. fri**ca**ssee _____ (**ca**sserole)
21. persist**ent** _____ (**rent**)
22. insist**ent** _____ (**rent**)
23. depend**ent** _____ (**rent**)
24. emba**rra**ssed _____ (**two r**obbers, Sing Sing, **ass**)
25. an**oi**nt _____ (**an oil**)

III. Decide on the missing crucial letter or letters, then rewrite the complete word.

1. emba—a—ed _____ (rr,ss)
2. ba—a—ion _____ (tt,l)
3. s—ge _____ (ie)
4. s—ze _____ (ei)
5. depend—ble _____ (a)
6. occu—nce _____ (rre)
7. d—spair _____ (e)
8. exhi—rate _____ (la)
9. abs—nce _____ (e)
10. rep—tition _____ (e)
11. b—ness _____ (usi)
12. d—scription _____ (e)
13. superintend—nt _____ (e)
14. a—oint _____ (n)
15. para—e— _____ (ll,l)
16. i—o—ulate _____ (n,c)
17. indispens—ble _____ (a)
18. fri—a—ee _____ (c,ss)
19. persist—nt _____ (e)
20. r—diculous _____ (i)
21. ho—iday _____ (l)
22. depend—nt _____ (e)
23. re—o—end _____ (c,mm)
24. insist—nt _____ (e)
25. vi—ious _____ (c)

A Footnote on Kinesthetic Training

In this chapter you have had a chance to write each new word at least four times—in addition you have written once again, in its correct pattern, every word from all previous mnemonics chapters.

This is kinesthetic practice of the most valuable kind—it is meaningful, combined with thinking, controlled by intellectual process.

You have doubtless heard the story of the fourth-grade

youngster who had developed the quaint but socially unacceptable habit of saying *I have went*. His teacher, somewhat confused about the principles of effective learning, decided that kinesthetic practice would cure her charge of his unfortunate lapse from correct usage. So she instructed him to stay after school and write one thousand times on the blackboards which surrounded the classroom the sentence *I have gone*. She warned the child that when she returned in the morning she would make a careful count, and left the school with the warm feeling that she finally had found a way to lick the problem.

The next morning she counted a full thousand carefully written *I have gone*'s; and found on her desk this significant note: "Dear teacher, I have done the work and I have went home."

Which proves that *meaningless* kinesthetic practice is a waste of time. Mere repetition will result in muscle fatigue, not in actual learning. But when you train your muscles to respond accurately to a practical situation, when you keep changing the situation while still calling for the same muscular response, then eventually your muscles can, in a sense, do their own thinking and react automatically and correctly.

Many of the activities you have learned in meaningful situations, and have repeated under changing stimuli, are now part of your "muscle thinking." If you drive a car, you make automatic muscular responses to the stimuli of familiar road conditions—the changing traffic lights, the actions of the car ahead, the erratic behavior of the death-defying pedestrians. When you buy in a familiar supermarket, you walk automatically to the proper shelves in response to the demands of your shopping list. In all these and similar cases you have, through meaningful practice, developed automatic and accurate muscular responses; you have driven your learning to lower-than-conscious levels and no longer need make conscious mental decisions.

And this is the result you are aiming for in your spelling—by writing a word a calculated number of times in response to changing situations you are letting your muscles as well as your mind become accustomed to the desirable patterns—eventually old and undesirable patterns will fade and be lost, and the new, correct patterns will be as much an integral part of your "muscle thinking" as the way you dress in the morning, drive your car, comb your hair, or do any other work at which you have developed skill.

So resist the temptation to merely *read* these chapters— fill every blank with the required words in your own handwriting, keep teaching your muscles to react accurately. From kinesthetic practice will come the self-assurance in spelling that you are working for.

12

When to Keep the
e After *c*

PROBLEMS

noti**ce**able *or* noti**ca**ble?
servi**ce**able *or* servi**ca**ble?

SOLUTION

C is a tricky letter.
And so it often makes for tricky and problem spellings.
There is a so-called "soft" and a so-called "hard" *c*.
Soft *c* has the sound of *s* in *sit*. Examples of soft *c* are:

city	notice
civil	mercy
pace	cylinder

Notice, then, that before the vowels *e, i*, and *y*,[1] *c* is usually soft. *E, i*, and *y* are therefore called "softening" vowels.

Hard *c* has the sound of *k* in *Kate*. Examples of hard *c* are:

cavern	panic
cost	closet
current	

---

[1] You will recall that we consider *y* the sixth vowel.

Notice, then, that before the vowels *a, o,* and *u, c* is usually hard. *A, o* and *u* are therefore called "hardening" vowels, *C* is also hard:

      1. as the *final* letter in a word; and
      2. before a consonant.

Keep these facts in mind, understand them thoroughly, and you will automatically solve a number of vexing problems.

Point 15
  C is usually soft
    —before *e* (*cent*)
    —before *i* (*cinch*)
    —before *y* (*cycle*)
  (*e, i* and *y* are "softening" vowels)

Point 16
  C is usually hard
    —before *a* (*car*)
    —before *o* (*come*)
    —before *u* (cur)
  (*a, o,* and *u* are "hardening" vowels)
    —as a final letter (*public*)
    —before consonants (*cry*)

The Vexing Problems
  Which is correct:

        notic**a**ble *or* noti**cea**ble?
        servi**ca**ble *or* servi**cea**ble?
        embra**ca**ble *or* embra**cea**ble?

We can now solve this type of problem easily and clearly.

Take the word *notice.* The *c* is soft (like *s*), coming before the softening vowel *e*.
Now take the misspelling *noticable.* Here, the *c* would be hard (like *k*), coming before the hardening vowel *a*. If

the *c* were hard, the word would be pronounced *NO-ti-ka-b'l*.

But of course the word is *not* pronounced *NO-ti-ka-b'l*. As everyone knows, it is pronounced *NO-ti-sa-b'l*.

So—

To keep the *c* soft, we must separate it from the hardening vowel *a*.

We separate the *c* from the hardening vowel *a* by retaining the softening final e of *notice*. Correct spelling:

noti**ce**able _____

Take the word *service*. The *c* is soft (like *s*), coming before the softening vowel *e*.

Now take the misspelling *servicable*. Here, the *c* would be hard (like *k*), coming before the hardening vowel *a*. If the *c* were hard, the word would be pronounced *SER-vik-a-b'l*. Again, as everyone knows, the correct pronunciation is not SER-vik-a-b'l, but *SER-vi-sa-b'l*.

So—

To keep the *c* soft, we must separate it from the hardening vowel *a*.

As in the case of *noticeable*, we separate the *c* from the hardening vowel *a* by retaining the softening final *e*. Correct spelling:

servi**ce**able _____

Note these words which contain a soft *c*.

embrace	trace	peace
lace	service	notice
replace	bounce	pronounce
	enforce	

If we wish to add *-able*, a suffix which starts with the hardening vowel *a*, we must retain the softening final *e* in each word.

embra**ce**able _____	boun**ce**able _____
la**ce**able _____	pea**ce**able _____
repla**ce**able _____	noti**ce**able _____

irreplaceable _____   pronounceable _____
traceable _____   enforceable _____
serviceable _____

(*Tracing, servicing*, etc., offer no problem—*i*, like *e*, is a softening vowel.)

Understand why the extra *e* is required, commit these words to visual memory, and you can eliminate another tricky and confusing problem in English spelling.

TEST YOURSELF

Add the suffix -*able* to the following verbs, rewriting the complete word. Decide, in each case, whether or not to retain the softening *e*.

1. enforce _____   (enforceable)
2. pronounce _____   (pronounceable)
3. embrace _____   (embraceable)
4. lace _____   (laceable)
5. seize _____   (seizable)
6. notice _____   (noticeable)
7. dispense _____   (dispensable)
8. peace _____   (peaceable)
9. replace _____   (replaceable)
10. use _____   (usable)
11. (ir)replace _____   (irreplaceable)
12. bounce _____   (bounceable)
13. believe _____   (believable)
14. service _____   (serviceable)
15. pleasure _____   (pleasurable)
16. trace _____   (traceable)
17. value _____   (valuable)
18. blame _____   (blamable)

13 *(Seventh Day, continued)*

When to Use a *k* After *c*

PROBLEMS

pani**cy** *or* pani**cky**?
froli**cing** *or* froli**cking**?
traffi**cer** *or* traffi**cker**?

SOLUTION

Now let us look at the other side of the coin—hard *c*'s which must be kept hard. When *c* is the final letter of a word, it is, as you know, pronounced like *k*.
For example:

zinc	panic
colic	picnic
frolic	traffic
physic	bivouac
mimic	shellac

Take the verb to *picnic*.
Suppose you wish to add the suffix *-er*, to denote *one who picnics*.
Your immediate temptation might be, in all innocence and directness, to write: *picnicer*.
But hold on!
C before e is soft, as you have learned.

The word would then be pronounced *PIK-niss-er*, obviously absurd.

We must do something to keep the ⁻*c* hard (like *k*) before a softening vowel (*e*).

So we do the obvious thing—we slip in a *k*.

And we get:

picnic**k**er _____

This may look awkward and unfamiliar—maybe unpleasant.

You will get used to it.

Other forms of *picnic* are spelled similarly, even though they may look similarly awkward, unfamiliar, and unpleasant.

picnic**k**ing _____ picnic**k**ed _____

And the same principle operates in other final -*c* words:

zinc**k**ing _____ frolic**k**er _____
coli**ck**y _____ physic**k**ing _____
frolic**k**ing _____ panic**k**ed _____
frolic**k**ed _____ shellac**k**ed _____
mimic**k**ed _____ traffic**k**ed _____
mimic**k**ing _____ traffic**k**ing _____
pani**ck**y _____ bivouac**k**ing _____
traffic**k**er _____ bivouac**k**ed _____

etc.

Point 17

When a word ends in *c*, like *picnic, frolic, panic*, or *traffic*—

And you wish to add -*ed*, -*er*, -*ing*, or -*y* (all softening vowels)—

First insert the letter *k* before these vowels—

And you will keep the pronunciation sane and sensible.

So watch your *c*'s.

To keep them soft before -*able*, retain the softening *e*.

To keep them hard before -*ed, -er, -ing,* or -*y*, insert *k*. And let your visual memory do the rest.

TEST YOURSELF

Add the required suffixes to each of the following words, rewriting the complete word.

I. Add -*ing* to:
1. frolic _____ (froli**ck**ing)
2. panic _____ (pani**ck**ing)
3. picnic _____ (picni**ck**ing)
4. traffic _____ (traffi**ck**ing)
5. zinc _____ (zin**ck**ing)
6. physic _____ (physi**ck**ing)
7. politic _____ (politi**ck**ing)
8. bivouac _____ (bivoua**ck**ing)
9. mimic _____ (mimi**ck**ing)
10. shellac _____ (shella**ck**ing)

II. Add -*er* to:
1. picnic _____ (picni**ck**er)
2. traffic _____ (traffi**ck**er)
3. bivouac _____ (bivoua**ck**er)
4. frolic _____ (froli**ck**er)

III. Add -*ed* to:
1. picnic _____ (picni**ck**ed)
2. frolic _____ (froli**ck**ed)
3. panic _____ (pani**ck**ed)
4. traffic _____ (traffi**ck**ed)
5. zinc _____ (zin**ck**ed)
6. physic _____ (physi**ck**ed)
7. politic _____ (politi**ck**ed)
8. bivouac _____ (bivoua**ck**ed)
9. mimic _____ (mimi**ck**ed)
10. shellac _____ (shella**ck**ed)

A Footnote on Zinc, Physic, Politic, and Bivouac

The words discussed in this chapter are all in common use with the exception of *bivouac*, and of *physic*, *politic*, and *zinc* as verbs.

A *bivouac* is a camp outdoors without tents, hence a kind of temporary shelter. The word is often heard in reference to military maneuvers, as when an army is *bivouacking* before battle, etc.

Physic, politic, and *zinc* are everyday words as nouns— but they are occasionally also used as verbs, as when we say that a mother believes in *physicking* her child at the first sign of a cold (that is, she pours great quantities of Ex-Lax, milk of magnesia, and castor oil into the un- happy youngster); or as when we say that the senator is *politicking* up and down the state (that is, repairing the political fences, as the handy cliché puts it, or making speeches that ask for re-election); or, finally, as when we say that we are in the process of *zincking* an object (that is, putting on a coat of *zinc*).

These verbs are picturesque usages and are gradually becoming more prevalent in speech and writing. Use them whenever you're so minded—and don't forget the very necessary *k* that keeps the *c* hard.

14

When to Keep the *e* After *g*

PROBLEMS

changeable *or* changable?
judgement *or* judgment?
mortgageor *or* mortgagor?

SOLUTION

You will recall that we considered *c* a tricky letter—because its pronunciation could be either "soft" or "hard."

Equally tricky is *g*—because it, too, can be either "soft" or "hard," and for the same reasons that operate in respect to the letter *c*.

Soft *g* has the sound of *j* in *just:*

advantage	spongy	judgment
change	gypsy	acknowledgment
changing	gin	

Notice, then, that *g*, like *c*, is soft before the softening vowels *e, i,* and *y*; and also when preceded by *d*.

Hard *g* has the sound of *g* in *glad:*

gas	gun	pig
gone	grin	ugly

Notice, then, that *g*, again like *c*, is hard before the hardening vowels, *a, o* and *u*; as the final letter in a word; and before a consonant.

Keep these facts in mind, understand them thoroughly, and you will again, as with the letter *c*, automatically solve a number of vexing problems.

Point 18
  G is usually soft
    —before *e* (*gem*)
    —before *i* (*gin*)
    —before *y* (*gymnasium*)
  (*e, i,* and *y* are softening vowels)

(Some short Anglo-Saxon words are obvious exceptions, such as *get, gift,* etc., but they won't trouble you.)
    —after *d* (*judgment*)

Point 19
  G is usually hard
    —before *a* (*gadget*)
    —before *o* (*got*)
    —before *u* (*guest, intrigue*)
  (*a, o,* and *u* are hardening vowels)
    —as a final letter (*slag, rug*)
    —before consonants (*green, glib*)

The Vexing Problems
  Which is correct:

> chan**gea**ble *or* chan**ga**ble?
> mana**gea**ble *or* mana**ga**ble?
> advanta**geo**us *or* advanta**go**us?
> abrid**gem**ent *or* abrid**gm**ent?

We can solve this type of problem quickly and successfully.

Take the word *charge*. The *g* is soft (pronounced like *j*).

We wish to add the suffix *-able*.

But *a* is a hardening vowel.

So we must keep the softening *e* between the *g* and the *a*.

Thus:

                chargeable _____

Similarly:

changeable _____	wageable _____
marriageable _____	salvageable _____
mortgageable _____	engageable _____
manageable _____	disengageable _____

O, like *a*, is a hardening vowel. If *g* must be pronounced soft before the suffix *-ous*, again we must keep the softening *e*.

Thus:

advantageous _____	courageous _____
disadvantageous _____	outrageous _____
gorgeous _____	

(This accounts for the strange spelling *George*, to differentiate it in pronunciation from *gorge*.)

Or take *judge, lodge, abridge, acknowledge*.

In each case the *g* is soft, both because of the softening vowel *e* and the preceding *d*.

Now *g* is usually hard before a consonant, as in *segment, ugly*, etc.

Nevertheless—

When we add *-ment* for the purpose of forming nouns from *judge, lodge, abridge*, and *acknowledge*, we eliminate the final *e*, relying on the preceding *d* to keep the *g* soft.

Thus (and these are the preferable spellings):

judgment _____	abridgment _____
lodgment _____	acknowledgment _____

(On the other hand, words like *disparage, encourage, discourage, enrage, engage*, do not contain a softening *d*—hence the *e* is retained before *-ment: disparagement, encouragement, discouragement, enragement, engagement*, etc. In fact, as you know, final *e* is regularly retained before *-ment* or any suffix beginning with a consonant.)

No exceptions to these principles?

Yes, there are two important types of exceptions to keep in mind.

Point 20

1. Despite the fact that *g* is usually hard before *o*, *mortgagor* (pronounced *MOR-ga-jer*) does not contain a softening *e*.

mortga**gor** _____

2. Although a preceding *d* keeps *g* soft in words like *acknowledgeable, bridgeable*, etc., we keep the softening *e* nevertheless, thus protecting the *g* both fore and aft.

acknowled**geable** _____   knowled**geable** _____
brid**geable** _____   abrid**geable** _____

Let me recapitulate briefly:

1. For soft g, retain the *e* before *-able* or *-ous*:

mana**geable** _____   outra**geous** _____
gorg**eous** _____   chang**eable** _____

2. After *dg*, preferably omit *e* before *-ment*:

jud**gment** _____   acknowled**gment** _____

3. Bear in mind the exceptions:

mortga**gor** _____   acknowle**dgeable** _____
knowle**dgeable** _____   brid**geable** _____

105

TEST YOURSELF

I. Rewrite the following words with an *-able* ending.
1. charge _____ (chargeable)
2. believe _____ (believable)
3. marriage _____ (marriageable)
4. bridge _____ (bridgeable)
5. acknowledge _____ (acknowledgeable)
6. change _____ (changeable)
7. pleasure _____ (pleasurable)
8. enrage _____ (enrageable)
9. manage _____ (manageable)
10. salvage _____ (salvageable)
11. engage _____ (engageable)
12. disengage _____ (disengageable)
13. value _____ (valuable)
14. mortgage _____ (mortgageable)

II. Rewrite the following words with an *-ous* ending.
1. advantage _____ (advantageous)
2. disadvantage _____ (disadvantageous)
3. courage _____ (courageous)
4. outrage _____ (outrageous)
5. (gorge) _____ (gorgeous)

III. Rewrite the following words with a *-ment* ending, using the preferable spelling.
1. judge _____ (judgment)
2. advertise _____ (advertisement)
3. lodge _____ (lodgment)
4. abridge _____ (abridgment)
5. disable _____ (disablement)
6. acknowledge _____ (acknowledgment)
7. disparage _____ (disparagement)
8. encourage _____ (encouragement)
9. discourage _____ (discouragement)

10. engage _____ (enga**gement**)
11. disengage _____ (disenga**gement**)

IV. Rewrite the following word with an *-or* ending.
   1. mortgage _____ (mortga**gor**)

MNEMONICS
Five (*Eighth Day, continued*)

PRETEST

1. alright *or* all right?
2. baloon *or* balloon?
3. pursuit *or* persuit?
4. sherrif *or* sheriff?
5. catagory *or* category?

MNEMONICS

1. (alright *or* all right?)

It is often said that this word has two spellings—the one most people use, and the correct one.

It is certainly logical enough to misspell the word in the pattern *alright*—it fits perfectly into the group of similar words: *already, altogether, also, almighty*, etc. But ALL RIGHT is the lone wolf, the rebel, the nonconformist in this group. It is acceptable only in the two-word, two-l pattern.

Of all the words in the English language (over 600,000 by last count) ALL RIGHT is without question the most frequently mispelled. Do not be surprised if you see it written *alright* occasionally in magazines and newspapers, frequently in letters written by otherwise civilized and erudite correspondents.

How can you remember its proper and accepted pattern? The mnemonic is simple—link it with its opposite, **ALL** WRONG. **ALL** RIGHT follows essentially the same form—two words, two **l**'s.

> *Correct Spelling:* **al**l right _____
> *Mnemonic:* **al**l wrong

2. (baloon *or* balloon?)

A BA**LL**OON, as even a young child knows, is usually a round object, a kind of BA**LL**. By linking BA**LL**OON to BA**LL**, you will automatically avoid the popular misspelling.

> *Correct Spelling:* ba**ll**oon _____
> *Mnemonic:* ba**ll**

3. (pursuit *or* persuit?)

Get this picture: A thief snatches your P**U**RSE—you tear after him in hot P**U**RSUIT.

> *Correct Spelling:* p**u**rsuit _____
> *Mnemonic:* p**u**rse

4. (sher**rif** *or* she**riff**?)

The problem in this word is the number of *r*'s and *f*'s. Keep in mind that a SHE**R**I**FF**'s duty is to protect respectable people against the **R**I**FF**-**R**A**FF**—hence one *r*, two *f*'s.

> *Correct Spelling:* she**riff**
> *Mnemonic:* **riff-raff**

(TA**R**I**FF**, by the way, follows the same pattern as SHE**R**I**FF**—one r, two *f*'s).

5. (cat**a**gory *or* cat**e**gory?)

The crucial letter in this word, as you can see, is the vowel following the *t*—is it an *a* or an *e*? One useful type of mnemonic is an easily spelled synonym of the problem word, a synonym that contains the correct crucial letters —in this case S**E**CTION, which is one of the synonyms of CAT**E**GORY, and which highlights the *e*.

Correct Spelling: category _____
Mnemonic: section

MNEMONICS CHART
Correct Pattern   *Mnemonic*

Correct Pattern	Mnemonic
all right _____	all wrong
balloon _____	ball
pursue _____	purse
sheriff _____	riff-raff
category _____	section

TEST YOURSELF

I. Check the correct pattern.
1. (a) alright,   (b) all right   (b)
2. (a) baloon,   (b) balloon   (b)
3. (a) pursuit,   (b) persuit   (a)
4. (a) sherrif,   (b) sheriff   (b)
5. (a) category,   (b) catagory   (a)
6. (a) tarrif,   (b) tariff   (b)

II. Recall the mnemonic for each word.
1. anoint _____ (an oil)
2. ridiculous _____ (ridicule)
3. business _____ (busy)
4. despair _____ (desperate)
5. balloon _____ (ball)
6. recommend _____ (commend)
7. repetition _____ (repeat)
8. holiday _____ (holy)
9. sheriff _____ (riff-raff)
10. all right _____ (all wrong)
11. embarrassed _____ (two robbers, Sing Sing, ass)
12. pursuit _____ (purse)
13. vicious _____ (vice)
14. category _____ (section)

15. absence _____ (absent)
16. description _____ (describe)
17. exhilarate _____ (hilarious)
18. indispens**able** _____ (**able** worker)
19. superintend**ent** _____ (**rent**)
20. se**ize** _____ (neck)
21. par**all**el _____ (**all** tracks)
22. insist**ent** _____ (**rent**)
23. depend**able** _____ (**able** worker)
24. fri**cass**ee _____ (**cass**erole)
25. depend**ent** _____ (**rent**)
26. s**ie**ge _____ (city)
27. persist**ent** _____ (**rent**)
28. occu**rr**ence _____ (cu**rr**ent event)
29. ba**tt**alion _____ (ba**ttle**)
30. in**oc**ulate _____ (in**ject**)

III. Decide on the missing crucial letters or letter, then rewrite the complete word.

1. i—o—ulate _____ (n,c)
2. a—right _____ (ll)
3. p—rsuit _____ (u)
4. occu—nce _____ (rre)
5. cat—gory _____ (e)
6. she—i— _____ (r,ff)
7. ba—oon _____ (ll)
8. indispens—ble _____ (a)
9. superintend—nt _____ (e)
10. depend—ble _____ (a)
11. persist—nt _____ (e)
12. ba—a—ion _____ (tt,l)
13. fri—a—ee _____ (c,ss)
14. re—o—end _____ (c,mm)
15. d—spair _____ (e)
16. insist—nt _____ (e)
17. para—e— _____ (ll,l)

18. a—oint _____ (n)
19. exhi—ration _____ (la)
20. bu—ness _____ (si)
21. depend—nt _____ (e)
22. s—ge _____ (ie)
23. vi—ious _____ (c)
24. abs—nce _____ (e)
25. r—diculous _____ (i)
26. s—ze _____ (ei)
27. ho—iday _____ (l)
28. d—scription _____ (e)
29. emba—a—ment _____ (rr,ss)
30. rep—tition _____ (e)

How to Manage Exceptions to the Dropped -*e* Rules

PROBLEMS

develo**pm**ent *or* develo**pem**ent?
arg**um**ent *or* arg**uem**ent?
tr**uly** *or* tr**uely**?
ey**ei**ng *or* ey**i**ng?

SOLUTION

You know that final *e* is *dropped* before a suffix beginning with a vowel—

(as in *blame—blamable*)

You know, also, that final *e* is *retained* if the suffix begins with a consonant—

(as in *care—careful*)

And you know that certain *c* and *g* words are conspicuous exceptions to these rules—

(as in *peace—peaceable; manage—manageable; judge—judgment*, etc.)

There are still other exceptions to, and side lights on, the dropped -*e* rules that it will pay us to consider.

1. How about *development*?

Words, like *statement, refinement, encouragement*, etc., lead many literate people to spell it *developement*—and at first glance this pattern looks far from impossible. However, realize that the original word is:

develop, *not* develope

There is no final *e* on the parent word, and so it is not a matter of keeping or dropping the *e*.

The only correct spelling, and the one you want to become visually accustomed to, is:

development _____

2. Other *-pment* words

The same principle operates in two other words. Note, in each case, that the parent word does *not* end in *e*.

PARENT WORD	*-ment* WORD
to envelop	envelopment _____
to equip	equipment _____

3. Six exceptions

There are important exceptions to the principle that *e* is dropped before a vowel, retained before a consonant. These are:

  1. wise + *-dom* = wisdom (no *e*) _____
  2. due + *-ly* = duly (no *e*) _____
  3. true + *-ly* = truly (no *e*) _____
  4. whole + *-ly* = wholly (no *e*) _____
  5. argue + *-ment* = argument (no *e*) _____
  6. awe + *-ful* = awful (no *e*) _____

(*Wholly*, if examined, looks peculiar, as does any word which does not seem to be pronounced the way it is spelled. But *wholly* is *whole* plus *-ly*, except that it is one of the six in which the *e* is dropped, resulting in *wholly*.)

  4. What about *full-of-holes*?

Hole ends in *e*. Add *y*, a vowel, and the result, by the principle we are discussing, should be *holy*. But *holy* means *pious, virtuous, sacred,* etc. So if we mean *full-of-holes,* we keep the *e,* and write *holey.* Thus:

The *holy* man's clothing was *holey.*

5. And *sincerely?*

Though *sincerely* follows our principle perfectly, for some odd reason the misspelling *sincerly* is popular. Note that we start with *sincere* which ends in a final *e.* We then add a consonant suffix, *-ly.* Therefore we keep the *e.*

sincerely _____

6. *Eyeing* or *eying?*

This word is a law unto itself. Either spelling is correct—*eying* or *eyeing,* with neither having preference over the other. The past is of course *eyed.*

7. Then there are *mile* and *line* and *nine.*

Mile and *line* are two more important exceptions. By the principle, the *e* should drop before *-age,* which begins with a vowel. But the *e* is kept.

mile + *-age* - mileage (pronounced *MY-lij*) _____
line + *-age* = lineage (pronounced *LIN-ee-ij*) _____

Lineage refers to someone's family tree—if the number of lines in print is meant, the spelling is *linage,* pronounced *LYNE-ij.*

As for *nine,* notice these forms:

nine + *-teen* = nineteen _____
nine + *-ty* = ninety _____
nine + *-th* = ninth _____

In *nineteen* and *ninety,* we follow the principle: keep the *e* before a consonant. In *ninth,* we have an exception—the *e* is dropped.

8. How about *acre?*

By our principle, *acre* + *-age* should produce *acrage.* Although the *e* of *acre* should be dropped before a vowel, it is, on the contrary, retained. Thus:

acre + -age = acreage (pronounced *AY-ker-ij*) ____

9. Finally, consider *stage* and *cage*.

Two more similar words could hardly be imagined— yet the first follows the dropped -*e* principle, the second is an exception, when the vowel y is added.

stage + -y = stagy _____
cage + -y = cagey _____

Of course, in forms like *staged, caged, staging*, and *caging*, the *e* is regularly dropped.

Let us now review, and commit to visual memory, the important problem words of this chapter.

1. development ____
2. envelopment ____
3. equipment ____
4. wisdom ____
5. duly ____
6. truly ____
7. wholly ____
8. argument ____
9. awful ____
10. holey ____
    (full of holes)
11. sincerely ____
12. eying or eyeing ____
13. mileage ____
14. lineage ____
    (*ancestry*)
15. linage ____
    (*lines*)
16. nineteen ____
17. ninety ____
18. ninth ____
19. acreage ____
20. stagy ____
21. cagey ____

TEST YOURSELF

Rewrite the following words with the indicated suffix.

1. develop + -*ment* _____ (development)
2. envelop + -*ment* _____ (envelopment)
3. equip + -*ment* _____ (equipment)
4. wise + -*dom* _____ (wisdom)
5. due + -*ly* _____ (duly)
6. true + -*ly* _____ (truly)
7. whole + -*ly* _____ (wholly)

8. argue + *-ment* _____ (arg**um**ent)
9. awe + *-ful* _____ (a**wf**ul)
10. hole + *-y* _____ (hol**ey**)
11. sincere + *-ly* _____ (sincer**el**y)
12. eye + *-ing* _____ (e**ye**ing or e**yi**ng)
13. mile + *-age* _____ (mil**ea**ge)
14. line + *-age* _____ (lin**ea**ge)
    (ancestry)
15. line + *-age* _____ (lin**a**ge)
    (*lines*)
16. nine + *-teen* _____ (nin**e**teen)
17. nine + *-ty* _____ (nin**e**ty)
18. nine + *-th* _____ (ni**nt**h)
19. acre + *-age* _____ (acr**ea**ge)
20. stage + *-y* _____ (sta**gy**)
21. cage + *-y* _____ (cag**ey**)

MNEMONICS
Six   *(Ninth Day, continued)*

PRETEST

1. occassional *or* occasional?
2. vacuum *or* vaccuum?
3. buy some stationary *or* stationery?
4. a man of principles *or* principals?
5. seperate *or* separate?

MNEMONICS

1. (occassional *or* occasional?)

Considering the pronunciation, there is no logical reason for misspelling this word—but misspelled it is, over and over, even by fairly sophisticated citizens of the country.

The popular, and *incorrect*, pattern contains a double *s*, thus: *occassional*; the purpose of an effective mnemonic will therefore be to highlight the need for one, and only one, *s* in the middle of the word.

This will not be difficult. Since spelling is tied up with pronunciation in OCCA**S**IONAL, let us do a little pronouncing.

Say these words aloud:

> treasure   pleasure
> measure   usual

You will note that the single *s* in these four words has the same sound exactly as the required single *s* in OCCASIONAL—a kind of liquid or voiced *sh* sound. Such a liquid *sh* sound is generally spelled with only one *s*, not two. Once you understand this principle, all temptations to use a double *s* in OCCASIONAL, OCCASIONALLY, or OCCASION will vanish.

> *Correct spelling:* occasional _____
>
> *Mnemonic:* pronunciation and spelling similar to words like *pleasure, measure, treasure, usual,* etc.

2. (vacuum *or* vaccuum?)

In this word, all logic tempts to a double *c*, and the probability is that you checked the second form. If so, you will be relieved to learn that you are in the numerous company of many other educated people who are similarly misled by logic; but as it happens, the correct pattern requires a single *c*—because VACUUM derives from the Latin verb *vacare*, to empty, from which same root also derive the English words *vacant, vacate, vacation, vacuous,* etc.

The obvious mnemonic, then, will be one that ties a confusing form to an easily spelled form of the same word—in this case, VACANT. VACANT means empty, and a VACUUM has been completely emptied of everything, including air.

> *Correct Spelling:* vacuum _____
>
> *Mnemonic:* vacant

3. (buy some stationary *or* stationery?)

Anything STATIONARY stands still—note the *a* in STATIONARY and in STAND.

On the other hand, STATIONERY means PAPER, envelopes, etc. Note the ER in STATIONERY and PAPER.

> *Correct Spellings* stationary (stand) _____
>
> *and Mnemonics:* stationery (paper) _____

4. (a man of princi**ple**s *or* princi**pal**s?)

A PRINCIP**LE** is a RU**LE**—note the *-le* ending on both words.

PRINCIP**A**L, on the other hand, means M**A**IN—note the *a* in both words.

Thus: A princip**le** in grammar (ru**le**)
   Business princip**le**s (ru**le**s)
   The princip**a**l reason (m**a**in)
   Interest on his princip**a**l (m**a**in money)
   Princip**a**l of a school (m**a**in teacher)
   Princip**a**ls in a play (m**a**in actors)
   Princip**a**ls in a business transaction (m**a**in people)

  Correct Spellings   princip**le** (ru**le**) _____
  and Mnemonics: princip**a**l (m**a**in) _____

5. (sep**e**rate *or* sep**a**rate?)

Adults usually spell this word correctly—most grade and high school students misspell it. The important letter is the one following the *p*. This crucial letter is *a*, not *e*.

To highlight this crucial letter, remember that SE**PA**-RATE means A**PA**RT—and associate the *pa* in both words.

  Correct Spelling: se**pa**rate _____
          (whether adjective or verb)
  Mnemonic: a**pa**rt

MNEMONICS CHART

Correct Pattern	Mnemonic
1. occa**s**ional _____	trea**s**ure, etc.
2. va**c**uum _____	va**c**ant
3. station**a**ry _____	st**a**nd
4. station**e**ry _____	pap**e**r
5. princip**le** _____	ru**le**
6. princip**a**l _____	m**a**in
7. se**pa**rate _____	a**pa**rt

TEST YOURSELF

I. Check the correct pattern.
1. (a) seperate, (b) separate   (b)
2. a man of (a) principle, (b) principal   (a)
3. something fixed is (a) stationery, (b) stationary   (b)
4. (a) vaccuum, (b) vacuum   (b)
5. (a) occasional, (b) occassional   (a)

II. Recall the mnemonic for each word.
1. stationery _____ (paper)
2. stationary _____ (stand)
3. principal _____ (main)
4. principle _____ (rule)
5. vacuum _____ (vacant)
6. absence _____ (absent)
7. repetition _____ (repeat)
8. pursuit _____ (purse)
9. separate _____ (apart)
10. balloon _____ (ball)
11. category _____ (section)
12. all right _____ (all wrong)
13. holiday _____ (holy)
14. despair _____ (desperate)
15. occasional _____ (measure)
16. business _____ (busy)
17. sheriff _____ (riff-raff)
18. ridiculous _____ (ridicule)
19. recommend _____ (commend)
20. description _____ (describe)

III. Decide on the crucial missing letter or letters, then
rewrite the complete word.
1. va—uum _____ (c)
2. station—ry (fixed) _____ (a)
3. p—rsuit _____ (u)
4. abs—nce _____ (e)

5. ho—iday _____ (l)
6. d—spair _____ (e)
7. station—ry (paper) _____ (e)
8. occa—ional _____ (s)
9. sep—rate _____ (a)
10. sher— _____ (iff)
11. a—right _____ (ll; two words)
12. re—o—end _____ (c,mm)
13. princip—(chief) _____ (al)
14. princip—(general truth) ____ (le)
15. d—scription _____ (e)
16. r—diculous _____ (i)
17. bu—ness _____ (si)
18. cat—gory _____ (e)
19. ba—oon _____ (ll)
20. rep—tition _____ (e)

How to Decide Between -*ly* and -*ally*

PROBLEMS

artisti**cly** *or* artisti**cally**?
publi**cly** *or* publi**cally**?
inciden**tly** *or* inciden**tally**?
coo**ly** *or* coo**lly**?

SOLUTION

The ending -*ly* changes an adjective into an adverb. For example:

ADJECTIVE	ADVERB	
sweet	sweetly	_____
close	closely	_____
clever	cleverly	_____
painful	painfully	_____
definite	definitely	_____
cool	coolly	_____
royal	royally	_____
beautiful	beautifully	_____

Now a close scrutiny of these forms will disclose important basic principles:

Point 21

The *-ly* ending is always added to the *adjective* form, never to any other form—

Point 22

If the adjective ends in *l*, *-ly* is tacked on to the complete adjective, producing an *-lly* form—

(as in *coolly, royally, beautifully, painfully, really,* etc.)

Let us see how these two points will solve most of our *-ly* problems.

Points 21 and 22 repeated

The ending *-ly* is always tacked on to the adjective form only. If the adjective form ends in *l*, the adverb will end in *-lly*.

Let me present a chart.

Charts are always forbidding, I know, and I have kept them at a minimum throughout this book.

But the following chart is the simplest, most effective way of driving home the basic principle that the *-ly* ending is added to the adjective only, never to the noun.

Examine the words and forms carefully, committing the adverbs to visual memory. And pay special attention to the sixth, seventh, eleventh, and fourteenth words—these starred adverbs are high on the list of commonly misspelled demons.

	NOUN	ADJECTIVE	ADVERB
1.	grace	gracious	graciously _____
2.	insanity	insane	insanely _____
3.	happiness	happy	happily[1] _____
4.	dizziness	dizzy	dizzily _____
5.	evidence	evident	evidently _____
*6.	accident	accidental	*accidentally _____
*7.	incident	incidental	*incidentally _____

[1] *y* changes to *i* before adding *-ly*.

124

8. ornament   ornamental   ornamentally _____
9. confidence   confident   confidently _____
10. confidence   confidential   confidentially _____
*11. reality   real   *really _____
12. beauty   beautiful   beautifully _____
13. experiment   experimental   experimentally _____
*14. coolness   cool   *coolly _____

Are these principles 100 per cent operative? No exceptions?

It would be naïve, as you realize by now, to look for exception-free principles. But in this instance the exceptions are few and at a minimum.

Exception 1

If an adjective ends in *double l*, one *l* is dropped before the ending -*ly* is added, and thus a triple *l* (*lll*) is avoided.

For example:

   dull—dully _____   ill—illy _____
   full—fully _____

Only the *double-l adjectives* are the exceptions. Words like the following end in only one *l* and therefore follow Point 22:

skillful—skillfully _____   youthful—youthfully _____
truthful—truthfully _____   cool-coolly _____
              etc.

Exception 2

The adjectives *whole, one, due*, and *true* drop the *e* before -*ly* is added (as we know from Chapter 15).

whole—wholly _____   due—duly _____
one—only _____   true—truly _____

(Of course, there are also the -*ble* adjectives which drop *e* before adding -*ly*, such as *possible—possibly, incredible—incredibly, terrible-terribly*, but these offer no spelling problem to the literate person.)

What if an adjective ends in *-ic*?

Every once in a while, as we sift through the principles and inconsistencies of English spelling, we chance upon a trend that is simple, straightforward, and practically free of exceptions.

One such trend concerns adjectives ending in *-ic*, such as:

academic	automatic
anemic	emphatic
aristocratic	lyric
puristic	prophetic
acoustic	scholastic

A problem often arises when we wish to write these and similar words in the adverbial form.

academi**cly** *or* academi**cally**?
puristi**cly** *or* puristi**cally**?
automati**cly** *or* automati**cally**?
artisti**cly** *or* artisti**cally**?
publi**cly** *or* publi**cally**?

These are happy questions to answer.

They are happy questions, because we find a short, to-the-point answer.

The answer is:

We always spell such words with the ending *-ally*.

Point 23

If an adjective ends in *-ic* always form the adverb by adding *-ally*.

Thus:

academic**ally** _____	automatic**ally** _____
anemic**ally** _____	emphatic**ally** _____
aristocratic**ally** _____	lyric**ally** _____
puristic**ally** _____	prophetic**ally** _____
acoustic**ally** _____	scholastic**ally** _____
artistic**ally** _____	etc.

Always?

Well, almost always.

Publicly is the only important exception.

Get used to the appearance of *publicly*. _____

Then cast all doubts aside. Any other adverb based on an -ic adjective will end in -ally.

athletic**ally** _____	phlegmatic**ally** _____
romantic**ally** _____	systematic**ally** _____

So we revise *Point 23* to read:

If an adjective ends in -*ic*, form the adverb by adding -*ally*, except in the case of *public*, to which only -*ly* is added.

Therefore—

When you wish to add -*ly*—

1. Remember to attach it to the adjective form only:

    (accidental) accident**ally** _____
    (incidental) incident**ally** _____

2. If the adjective ends in *l*, add -*ly* directly:

(cool) coo**lly** _____	(royal) roya**lly** _____
(real) rea**lly** _____	(skillful) skillfu**lly** _____

3. Remember the exceptions:

du**lly** _____	on**ly** _____
fu**lly** _____	du**ly** _____
who**lly** _____	tru**ly** _____

4. If the adjective ends in -*ic*, add -*ally*:

rustic**ally** _____	puristic**ally** _____
artistic**ally** _____	romantic**ally** _____

5. Remember the exception:

        public**ly** _____

With a full understanding of Points 21–23, plus a sharp visual memory of the words to which these points apply, you can no longer go wrong on any -*ly* word.

TEST YOURSELF

Write the adverb (-*ly*) form for the following words.

1. artistic _____ (artisti**ca**lly)
2. public _____ (publi**cly**)
3. incident _____ (incident**a**lly)
4. cool _____ (coo**lly**)
5. accident _____ (accident**a**lly)
6. painful _____ (painfu**lly**)
7. dull _____ (du**lly**)
8. full _____ (fu**lly**)
9. royal _____ (roya**lly**)
10. real _____ (rea**lly**)
11. happy _____ (happi**ly**)
12. evident _____ (evident**ly**)
13. confident _____ (confident**ly**)
14. confidential _____ (confidenti**a**lly)
15. experimental _____ (experiment**a**lly)
16. monumental _____ (monument**a**lly)
17. breezy _____ (breezi**ly**)
18. skillful _____ (skillfu**lly**)
19. truthful _____ (truthfu**lly**)
20. whole _____ (who**lly**)
21. one _____ (o**nly**)
22. due _____ (du**ly**)
23. true _____ (tru**ly**)
24. academic _____ (academi**ca**lly)
25. rustic _____ (rusti**ca**lly)
26. aristocratic _____ (aristocrati**ca**lly)
27. acoustic _____ (acousti**ca**lly)
28. lyric _____ (lyri**ca**lly)
29. romantic _____ (romanti**ca**lly)
30. systematic _____ (systemati**ca**lly)
31. analytic _____ (analyti**ca**lly)

Second Review

We have dealt in Chapters 11–16, with six broad groups of spelling demons—

I. WORDS WHICH DROP A FINAL *e* WHEN A SUFFIX BEGINNING WITH A VOWEL IS ADDED.

come—coming _____   desire—desirable _____
love—lovable _____   stone—stony _____
like—likable _____   bone—bony _____
                   etc.

II. WORDS WHICH RETAIN A FINAL *e* AFTER THE LETTER *c* WHEN THE SUFFIX *-able* IS ADDED.

noti**ce**able _____   pea**ce**able _____
servi**ce**able _____   pronoun**ce**able _____
irrepla**ce**able _____   tra**ce**able _____
                   etc.

III. WORDS WHICH INSERT A *-k* AFTER FINAL *c* WHEN A SUFFIX BEGINNING WITH *e*, *i* OR *y* IS ADDED.

panic—panic**k**y _____   mimic—mimic**k**ed _____
traffic—traffic**k**er _____   picnic—picnic**k**ing _____
frolic—frolic**k**ing _____   physic—physic**k**ed _____
                   etc.

IV. WORDS WHICH RETAIN A FINAL *e* AFTER THE LETTER *g* WHEN THE SUFFIX *-able* OR *-ous* IS ADDED.

changeable _____   marriageable _____
manageable _____   salvageable _____
outrageous _____   courageous _____
               etc.

V. WORDS WHICH PREFERABLY DROP FINAL *e* AFTER *dg* WHEN *-ment* IS ADDED.

judgment _____   abridgment _____
lodgment _____   acknowledgment _____
               etc.

VI. ADJECTIVES WHICH END IN *-ic* AND ADD *-ally* FOR ADVERBIAL FORMS.

rustic—rustically _____   analytic—analytically ____
artistic—artistically _____   lyric—lyrically _____
               etc.

In addition, we have discussed a number of other basic principles:

1. Final *-e* is retained when a suffix beginning with a consonant is added:

care—careful _____   like—likeness _____
vague—vaguely _____   refine—refinement _____
               etc.

2. If a word ends in *-dge*, final *-e* is retained before adding *-able*, even though a preceding *d* normally keeps a *g* soft:

knowledgeable _____   abridgeable _____
               etc.

3. No *-e* is added before *-ment* if the original word ended in a consonant:

develop—develo**pm**ent ____   equip—equi**pm**ent _____
envelop—envelo**pm**ent ____   embarrass—
                                      embarra**ss**ment _____
                etc.

4. Certain exceptional words drop final -e when a suffix beginning with a consonant is added:

wise—wi**sd**om _____   whole—who**ll**y _____
due—**d**u**l**y _____   argue—arg**um**ent _____
true—tr**ul**y _____   awe—a**wf**ul _____

5. The word *hole* retains final -e before -y is added to distinguish it from *holy*:

(full of holes) hol**ey** ____   (pious) hol**y** _____

6. *Mile, line,* and *acre* retain final -e before adding *-age*:

mil**e**age _____   lin**e**age _____
*acr***e**age _____   (if it means *family
                              descent,* otherwise *linage)*

7. *Nine* drops final -e before *-th,* retains it before *-teen* and *-ty.*

ni**nth** _____   nin**e**teen _____
nin**ety** _____

8. *Stage* drops final -e before adding *-y; cage* retains it.

stage—sta**gy** _____   cage—cag**ey** _____

9. *Eye* may optionally either drop or retain final -e before *-ing*:

eying _____   or eyeing _____

10. If an adjective ends in *l,* the adverb will end in *-lly*:

accident**al**—   incident**al**—
   accident**ally** _____   incident**ally** _____
coo**l**—coo**ll**y _____   real—rea**ll**y _____
                etc.

11. If an adjective ends in *ll*, the adverbs end in *-lly*:

full-fully _____   dull—dully _____

etc.

12. *Public* alone, among the hundreds of common *-ic* adjectives, adds only *-ly* to form an adverb:

public—publicly _____

13. When *-or* is added to mortgage, final *-e* is dropped:

mortgagor _____

SECOND REVIEW TEST

I. Add the indicated suffix to each word, rewriting in the blank space.

1. like + *-able* _____ (likable)
2. value + *-able* _____ (valuable)
3. desire + *-able* _____ (desirable)
4. love + *-able* _____ (lovable)
5. give + *-ing* _____ (giving)
6. size + *-able* _____ (sizable)
7. argue + *-ing* _____ (arguing)
8. care + *-ful* _____ (careful)
9. notice + *-able* _____ (noticeable)
10. service + *-able* _____ (serviceable)
11. enforce + *-able* _____ (enforceable)
12. enforce + *-ment* _____ (enforcement)
13. embrace + *-ing* _____ (embracing)
14. use + *-able* _____ (usable)
15. panic + *-y* _____ (panicky)
16. mimic + *-ry* _____ (mimicry)
17. mimic + *-ing* _____ (mimicking)
18. frolic + *-ed* _____ (frolicked)
19. colic + *-y* _____ (colicky)
20. change + *-able* _____ (changeable)

21. knowledge + -able _____ (knowledgeable)
22. mortgage + -or _____ (mortgagor)
23. judge + -ment _____ (judgment)
24. acknowledge + -ment _____ (acknowledgment)
25. engage + -ment _____ (engagement)
26. outrage + -ous _____ (outrageous)
27. courage + -ous _____ (courageous)
28. develop + -ment _____ (development)
29. equip + -ment _____ (equipment)
30. wise + -dom _____ (wisdom)
31. due + -ly _____ (duly)
32. true + -ly _____ (truly)
33. whole + -ly _____ (wholly)
34. argue + -ment _____ (argument)
35. awe + -ful _____ (awful)
36. hole + -y _____ (holey)
37. sincere + -ly _____ (sincerely)
38. mile + -age _____ (mileage)
39. line + -age _____ (lineage)
(ancestry)
40. line + -age _____ (linage)
(lines in print)
41. nine + -th _____ (ninth)
42. nine + -ty _____ (ninety)
43. nine + -teen _____ (nineteen)
44. acre + -age _____ (acreage)
45. stage + -y _____ (stagy)
46. cage + -y _____ (cagey)
47. accident + -ly _____ (accidentally)
48. incident + -ly _____ (incidentally)
49. cool + -ly _____ (coolly)
50. public + -ly _____ (publicly)

18

How to Decide Between *C* and *S* in the Ending of a Word

PROBLEMS

prophecy *or* prophesy?
ecstacy *or* ecstasy?
pretence *or* pretense?
licence *or* license?

SOLUTION

No literate Spaniard ever has trouble with the spelling of Spanish words.

Ditto for the literate Italian.

For in these two languages, among others, a word is generally spelled the way it sounds, and sounds the way it is spelled.

Not so, as you have long since discovered, in English.

The letter *s*, for example, may have any number of sounds.

It may sound like *sh*, as in *sure* and *sugar*.

It may sound like *z*, as in *miser*.

It may sound like *zh*, as in *leisure* or *measure*.

It can be silent, as in *viscount*.

Or take *c*. It can be hard, as in *cat*; soft, as in *city*; like a *ch*, as in *cello*; like *sh*, as in *appreciate*; or even silent, as in *indict*.

rds: *ecstasy,* *hypocrisy,* *idiosyncrasy,* and

iate between *prophesy* and *prophecy* by using
n as a verb, the *-cy* form as a noun. Remem-
ophesy is pronounced *PROFF-e-sigh, prophecy*
ced *PROFF-e-see.*

sing between *-ence* and *-ense,* again bear in
special words: *pretense, offense, defense,* and

is background, you should normally not en-
iy problems. Other *-cy-sy* and *-ence-ense* forms
ver cause trouble.

TEST YOURSELF

y or *-sy,* as required, to the following forms,
the complete word.

ta— _____	(sy)
osyncra— _____	(sy)
osta— _____	(sy)
pocri— _____	(sy)
can— _____	(cy)
urte— _____	(sy)
prophe— _____	(sy)
erb)	
foolish prophe— _____	(cy)
noun)	
iva— _____	(cy)
iploma— _____	(cy)

How to Decide Between *c* and *s* in the Ending of a Word

That's just a small indication of what you're up against
when you attempt to spell English words.

And it works the other way around.

A single sound can have two or more different spellings. The sound "seed," as you know, may be spelled
-sede, as in *supersede;* *-cede* as in *accede;* *-ceed* as in
proceed. Sea and *see* are identical in sound, and so are
there and *their* and *they're; to, too, two; been* and *bin;*
stationary and *stationery; die* and *dye;* and so on and on
and on.

A similar occurrence (and therein lies the problem) is
found in words which end with the syllable that sounds
like "see."

For example, *vacancy.*

Vacancy ends in *-cy.*

For further example, *ecstasy.*

Ecstasy, with the same final sound, ends in *-sy.*

How can we ever know which is which?

The problem begins to sound complicated.

But even a complicated problem can be made simple
and can be quickly and effectively solved if we attack it
dynamically.

The *-cy-or-sy* problem is no exception.

First let us discover exactly where the problem occurs.

*No normal speller is ever tempted to write -sy where -cy
is required.* There are words, however, in which he is
tempted to make the opposite substitution—using *-cy* in
place of the correct *-sy.*

How many such words?

Generally no more than four.

These four, acceptable only with an *-sy* ending, are:

ecstasy _____   hypocrisy _____
idiosyncrasy _____   apostasy _____

(An *apostate* has forsaken his religion, faith, principles,
or political affiliations. He is a kind of turncoat, a traitor
to his previous cause or beliefs. *Apostasy,* then, is the
noun that describes the apostate's desertion.)

Ecstasy, idiosyncrasy, hypocrisy, and *apostasy* are of

course not by any means the only English words ending in -sy—but they are the only ones likely to cause confusion or to be unconsciously misspelled. Words like *pleurisy, heresy, argosy, courtesy, fantasy* also end in -sy—but there is no tendency even among comparatively poor spellers to end them with -cy.

So an apparently complicated problem is in actuality relatively simple.

Become visually and kinesthetically adjusted to the pattern of four words:

ecstasy _____   hypocrisy _____
idiosyncrasy _____   apostasy _____

And then set your doubts at rest. In all other words you will naturally use the correct ending.

Speaking of -sy and -cy, this is as good a time as any to consider the confusing words *prophesy* and *prophecy*.

> *prophesy* is pronounced *PROFF-e-sigh*
> *prophecy* is pronounced *PROFF-e-see*

Prophesy (*PROFF-e-sigh*) is a verb, and has the usual verb forms:

To *prophesy* a real-estate boom.
He *prophesied* a real-estate boom. (*PROFF-e-sighed*)
She *prophesies* a real-estate boom. (*PROFF-e-sighs*)
We are *prophesying* a real-estate boom. (*PROFF-e-sigh-ing*)

Prophecy (*PROFF-e-see*) is a noun, with the usual plural form:
One *prophecy* (*PROFF-e-see*)
Many *prophecies* (*PROFF-e-sees*)
What about *prophecize*?
There is simply no such word—although it may occasionaly be heard as an erroneous substitute for the verb to *prophesy*.

As in the case of -cy and -sy, the problem of whether to end a word with -ence or -ense is deceptively complicated, but actually very simple.

How to Decide Between c and s

Most words in which there is ___ end in -ence: benevolence, cons ___ rience, etc., etc. And rarely ___ where -ence is required.

But in four special instances, ___ tion to substitute -ence for the p ___ These four instances are:

pretense _____   de ___
offense _____   lic ___

(British usage, strangely enoug ___ ing in these words—but the only ___ can spelling of these forms is -ens ___

You will have no difficulty sepa ___ *defense*, and *license* from the vast ___ if you consider their easily spelled ___

pretense—pretension   de ___
offense—offensive   lic ___

Here again, you need only beco ___ thetically adjusted to four special v ___ is automatically solved. In all oth ___ and without hesitation make the c ___ -ence and -ense.

For most words in which a cho ___ -ence—

And the few other words (besi ___ have mentioned) which end in -e ___ *intense, dispense, suspense*, etc.) ca ___

Let me offer the special cases ___ visual and kinesthetic practice.

pretense _____   defe ___
offense _____   licen ___

We can now sum up the solution ___ lems by formulating four basic prin ___

Point 24
In choosing between -cy and -sy ___

specia ___
aposta ___

Point ___
Dif ___
the -s ___
ber th ___
is pro ___

Point ___
In ___
mind ___
license ___

Point ___
Wit ___
counte ___
rarely ___

_____

_____

I. Ad ___
rewrit ___
1.
2.
3.
4.
5.
6.
7.

8.

9.
10.

II. Add *-ce* or *-se* to the following forms, rewriting the complete word.

1. defen— _____ (se)
2. offen— _____ (se)
3. licen— _____ (se)
4. preten— _____ (se)
5. suspen— _____ (se)
6. expen— _____ (se)
7. experien— _____ (ce)
8. impertinen— _____ (ce)
9. dispen— _____ (se)
10. inten— _____ (se)

19 *(Twelfth Day, continued)*

How to Decide Between *-ify* and *-efy*

PROBLEMS

liquify *or* liquefy?
rarify *or* rarefy?
stupify *or* stupefy?
putrify *or* putrefy?

SOLUTION

The four problem words of this chapter are among the forms generally misspelled by even the most literate and educated of writers.

What makes these words so troublesome? Why do so many educated people misspell them without any realization of error? (You will find many stubborn souls so certain that the *incorrect* form is correct that they will bet money on it!)

The answer is simple.

If there is a choice, practically every similar word ends in *-ify*, not *-efy*.

For instance:

classify	edify
codify	qualify
crucify	testify

And so on, scores and scores of them.

Every word, that is, *except the four problem words that start this chapter*.

Point 28

These four, and only these four among problem words, end in -efy.[1]

1. liquefy _____   3. stupefy _____
2. rarefy _____   4. putrefy _____

And of course other forms of these words follow the same pattern.

liquefying _____	rarefied _____
liquefied _____	rarefies _____
liquefies _____	stupefying _____
liquefaction _____	stupefied _____
rarefying _____	stupefies _____
stupefaction _____	putrefies _____
putrefying _____	putrefaction _____
putrefied _____	etc.

How can you remember that these four alone end in *-efy*?

There will be no difficulty. A few moments devoted to committing them to visual memory and to kinesthetic practice will solve your problem.

For exceptions, as you have probably learned, are easy to remember.

(Remember *supersede, procedure, paralyze, analyze, leisure, weird, seize, mortgagor*, etc.?)

Keep *liquefy, rarefy, stupefy*, and *putrefy* in mind, not so that you can repeat them in order, necessarily, but only so that you will recall them as exceptions when you have to write them—

---

[1]There are also, for example, *defy*, which offers no spelling problem, and *torrefy*, a rather obscure word meaning *to subject to heat. Torrify*, however, is also acceptable.

And then spell, as you naturally would anyway, any other word with the natural ending -*ify*.

TEST YOURSELF

Decide whether -*efy* or -*ify* is required to complete each form, then rewrite the complete word in the space provided.

1. oss— _____ (ify)
2. rat— _____ (ify)
3. liqu— _____ (efy)
4. spec— _____ (ify)
5. stup— _____ (efy)
6. putr— _____ (efy)
7. pac— _____ (ify)
8. fort— _____ (ify)
9. rar— _____ (efy)
10. rect— _____ (ify)

A Footnote on Derivations

As we have often decided, an odd or exceptional spelling is generally caused by the foreign root on which an English word is built. And three of the four -*efy* patterns on this chapter are so caused.

1. *Liquefy* comes from Latin *liquere*, to be fluid, and the *e* after the *qu* in the Latin root is retained. As for *liquid*, only the *liqu* of the Latin root was used, and the common -*id* suffix added. It's confusing, unjust, and perhaps even contradictory—but, as I have often had to say in unconvincing justification, that's the way it is and there's little we can do about it.

2. *Putrefy* comes from Latin *putrere*, to be rotten, and again the *e* of the classical root is retained before the -*fy* suffix. *Putrid*, like *liquid*, adds -*id* to the first four letters of the original root. But *putrescent*, which means *becoming rotten*, has that same crucial *e* after the *r*.

3. *Rarefy* is a truly bastardized and adulterated spell-

ing. The root on which the word is built is Latin *rarus*, thin, with no *e* in evidence. Somehow the *e* that ends the English *rare* remained firmly attached when *-fy* was added. Yet *purify*, from Latin *purus*, contains *i* before *-fy*, despite the English word *pure*. Illogical? English spelling always is.

4. *Stupefy* comes from Latin *stupere*, to be stunned, and again the *e* of the root is kept before *-fy*. *Stupid* falls into the same class as *liquid* and *putrid*.

The suffix *-fy*, by the way, is from the Latin verb *facere*, to make. So *liquefy* is *to make liquid; putrefy* is *to make or become rotten*; stupefy is *to make insensible; pacify* is *to make peaceful*; *fortify* is *to make strong*, and so on.

MNEMONICS
Seven *(Twelfth Day, continued)*

PRETEST

1. acce**ll**erate *or* acce**l**erate?
2. de**v**ise *or* di**v**ise?
3. ir**r**idescent *or* ir**i**descent?
4. tranqui**l**ity *or* tranqui**ll**ity?
5. gramm**e**r *or* gramm**a**r?

MNEMONICS

1. (acce**ll**erate *or* acce**l**erate?)

There is some temptation here to double the *l*, as the second syllable receives the accent. The correct spelling is best remembered by analogy with another form, CELERITY. ACCELERATE means *to speed up*, CELERITY means *speed*—both are derived from the same Latin root, *celer*, fast.

> *Correct Spelling:* accelerate _____
> *Mnemonic:* celerity

2. (de**v**ise *or* di**v**ise?)

This demon sounds like *divise*, and by analogy with *divide* seems an eminently sensible pattern. However, only DEVISE is correct; to remember the crucial *e*, use a mnemonic that ties a difficult form of a word to an easily spelled form, as we did in DESCRIPTION—DESCRIBE.

The adjective form of DEVISE is DEVIOUS, impossible to misspell since the pronunciation (*DEE-ve-us*) demands an *e* for the first vowel.

> *Correct Spelling:* devise _____
> *Mnemonic:* devious

(The noun form, DEVICE, has the same second letter as DEVISE.)

3. (irridescent *or* iridescent?)

This word means *having a rainbow of colors*, and derives from the Greek root *iris*, rainbow. There is also an *iris* in the eye, derived from the same root; and because of the pronunciation of *iris* (*EYE-ris*), there is no temptation to double the *r*. In IRIDESCENT (pronounced *ir-i-DESS-ent*), the pronunciation does tempt to a double *r*, but the mnemonic IRIS will help you avoid that common pitfall.

> *Correct Spelling:* iridescent _____
> *Mnemonic:* iris

4. (tranquility *or* tranquillity?)

The preferable spelling contains a double *l*—think that in the old days life had (so they say) far more TRANQUILLITY than today; and those were the days, also, when people wrote with QUILLS rather than ball-point pens.

> *Preferable Spelling:* tranquillity _____
> *Mnemonic:* quill

The base word, of course, is spelled TRANQUIL.)

5. (grammer *or* grammar?)

The pronunciation is indeed *GRAM-mer*, and so tempts to misspelling. Keep in mind that poor GRAMMAR MARS your speech.

> *Correct Spelling:* grammar _____
> *Mnemonic:* mar

MNEMONICS CHART

Correct Pattern	*Mnemonic*
1. acce**ler**ate	ce**ler**ity
2. de**vi**se	de**vi**ous
3. **iri**descent	**iri**s
4. tran**quill**ity	**quill**
5. gram**mar**	**mar**

TEST YOURSELF

I. Check the correct or preferable pattern.

1. (a) grammer,	(b) grammar		(b)
2. (a) accellerate,	(b) accelerate		(b)
3. (a) tranquillity,	(b) tranquility		(a)
4. (a) divise,	(b) devise		(b)
5. (a) irridescent,	(b) iridescent		(b)

II. Recall the mnemonic for each word.

1. gram**mar**	(**mar**)
2. **iri**descent	(**iri**s)
3. acce**ler**ate	(ce**ler**ity)
4. de**vi**se	(de**vi**ous)
5. tran**quill**ity	(**quill**)
6. ba**ll**oon	(ba**ll**)
7. cat**e**gory	(s**e**ction)
8. station**e**ry	(pap**e**r)
9. abs**e**nce	(abs**e**nt)
10. p**ur**suit	(p**ur**se)
11. occa**s**ional	(mea**s**ure)
12. va**c**uum	(va**c**ant)
13. sheri**ff**	(ri**ff**-ra**ff**)
14. ho**l**iday	(ho**l**y)
15. station**a**ry	(st**a**nd)
16. princip**al**	(m**a**in)
17. a**ll** right	(a**ll** wrong)
18. princip**le**	(ru**le**)

19. sep**a**rate _____ (ap**a**rt)
20. de**s**pair _____ (de**s**perate)

III. Decide on the crucial missing letters, then rewrite the complete word.

1. d—vise _____ (e)
2. station—ry (supplies) _____ (e)
3. p—rsuit _____ (u)
4. va—uum _____ (c)
5. sher— _____ (iff)
6. occa—ional _____ (s)
7. ho—iday _____ (l)
8. gramm—r _____ (a)
9. abs—nce _____ (e)
10. ba—oon _____ (ll)
11. princip— (chief) _____ (al)
12. a—right _____ (ll)
13. i—idescent _____ (r)
14. d—spair _____ (e)
15. princip— (truth) _____ (le)
16. acce—erate _____ (l)
17. cat—gory _____ (e)
18. station—ry (fixed) _____ (a)
19. sep—rate _____ (a)
20. tranqui—ity _____ (ll)

20

When to Double a Consonant and When to Leave It Alone

PROBLEM

gases *or* gasses?
buses *or* busses?
quizes *or* quizzes?

SOLUTION

Of course you can spell *gas.*

You can spell *bus.*

You can spell *quiz, regret, refer, travel, begin, equip.*

There is usually no problem in these words—they are spelled pretty much the way they are pronounced, a refreshing and (you may feel) a relatively rare circumstance.

The problem arises when you want to use a longer form of any of these or similar words: *gases* or *gasses? buses* or *busses? quizes* or *quizzes? regretable* or *regrettable? refering* or *referring? traveler* or *traveller? begining* or *beginning? equiped* or *equipped?*

And it is a problem that arises again and again.

In fact, it is one of the commonest and most plaguing of spelling problems—*when to double a consonant and when to leave it alone.*

You know what a consonant is? A consonant is any of twenty letters of the alphabet: *b, c, d, f, g, h, j, k, l, m, n, p, q, r, s, t, v, w, x, z.*

In other words, it is any letter other than one of the six vowels: *a, e, i, o, u, y*. (You will recall that we consider *y* the sixth vowel.)

There is a comparatively reliable but painfully complicated principle that covers the problem.

It is, I repeat, a painfully complicated principle—and if I were so reckless as to present it baldly and without considerable preparation you might run the risk of becoming hopelessly confused and discouraged.

So valuable is the principle, however; so easy to apply when it is clearly and thoroughly understood; and so far-reaching in its influence over many hundreds of words which perplex the average speller, that we want to explore it deeply and completely.

So we shall take the principle apart, study it piece by piece, understand every ramification of it, apply it in scores of practical situations, and thereby become so familiar with it that its complexity will vanish and all possibility of attendant pain will be avoided.

First

Our doubling principle applies largely to *verbs*.

A *verb*, as you may know, is a word that shows action, like

to grab	to stop
to swim	to bag
to run	to hop
to blur	to twit
to quiz	to trot

The ten verbs I have offered as examples contain, it so happens, only one syllable. But the principle applies just as effectively to verbs of any number of syllables, though most of the examples will be one to three syllables in length. For example:

to control	to travel
to repel	to develop
to regret	to inhibit
to refer	to disinter
to benefit	

Second

Our interest in this chapter will for a time center on *one-syllable verbs* of a very special type. You have already been exposed to ten examples of this type of verb (*grab, swim, run, trot*, etc.) and possibly you have noticed a common and most important element.

Each such verb ended in a single consonant.

Here are some similar verbs; the single, final consonant is printed in heavy type.

to qui**t**   to ski**p**
to pla**n**   to dru**m**
to cha**r**   to we**t**

Now examine once again the sixteen one-syllable verbs I have offered.

You will notice a second common and important element—*each final single consonant is preceded by a single vowel*. This single vowel is printed in heavy type.

gr**a**b   tw**i**t
sw**i**m   tr**o**t
r**u**n   qu**i**t[1]
bl**u**r   pl**a**n
qu**i**z[1]   ch**a**r
st**o**p   sk**i**p
b**a**g   dr**u**m
h**o**p   w**e**t

All right—we've got two important points to consider. If a one-syllable verb

1. *ends in a single consonant*
2. *preceded by a single vowel*

Then—
You double the final consonant before adding a suffix.

---

[1]In the case of *quiz* and *quit*, the *u* is pronounced like W (*KWIZ, KWIT*) and so does not function as a vowel.

When to Double a Consonant and When to Leave It Alone

Any kind of suffix?

No—but don't worry about that for just a moment.

Now watch how we double the final consonant before adding a suffix.

grab + *-ing* - grabbing _____

swim + *-er* = swimmer _____

run + *-ing* - running _____

blur + *-ed* = blurred _____

quiz + *-es* = quizzes[2] _____

quiz + *-ed* = quizzed[2] _____

quiz + *-ing* = quizzing[2] _____

stop + *-ing* = stopping _____

hop + *-ing* = hopping _____

twit + *-ing* = twitting _____

trot + *-er* = trotter _____

quit + *-er* = quitter _____

plan + *-ed* = planned _____

char + *-ed* = charred _____

skip + *-ed* = skipped _____

drum + *-er* = drummer _____

wet + *-ing* - wetting _____

I have asked whether this principle operates when any kind of suffix is added—and I have answered no, not any kind.

The suffixes we have added in the preceding list were *-ing, -ed, -es,* or *-er.*

In short, suffixes starting with a vowel.

Now this is all simple enough, and probably the only words you might have misspelled, if any, were *quizzes, quizzed* and *quizzing*—but don't become impatient. This material, so far, is all introductory, intended as essential preparation for harder and more important applications of the doubling principle.

---

[2]Of all these and similar words, *quizzes, quizzed* and *quizzing* are the most likely to be misspelled, often appearing, incorrectly, with a single z.

If we go very slow, bit by bit, if we take it easy, adequately preparing every step of the way, you will shortly, and painlessly, become an expert on the complete and complicated doubling principle.

So let us now state what we know so far.

Point 29

If a one-syllable word (usually a verb)—
Ends in a *single* consonant—
(like grab)
Preceded by a *single* vowel—
(grab)
You double the final consonant—
Before adding a suffix—
Which begins with a vowel.
(grab + *-ing* = grabbing).

(You see how involved it already sounds—but you understand it so far because of the careful, step-by-step preparation. And this is only *part* of the doubling principle!)

If a suffix begins with a consonant, such as *-ness*, *-ly*, *-ful*, or *-ment*, the principle does not hold.

wet + -ness = wetness
thin + -ness = thinness

(We have not doubled the final *n*, but only combined the *n* of *thin* with the *n* of *-ness*).

man + -ly = manly
drum + -ful = drumful
ship + -ment = shipment

Now consider, as special cases (in English spelling there are almost always special cases)—

gas and *bus*

Both *gas* and *bus* end in single consonants preceded by single vowels.

In the case of *gas*, when we add *-ed* or *-ing*, we follow

the doubling principle exactly as described—we double
the *s*.

gassed _____

gassing _____

But—

(And now you will further understand why English
spelling is such a headache, why it causes so much
insecurity.)

With other suffixes, such as *-es, -eous, -ify, we do not
double the s*—even though these suffixes also, like *-ed*
and *-ing*, start with a vowel.

gases _____

gaseous _____

   (pronounced *GAS-ee-us*)

gasify _____

gasifiable _____

gasifier _____

gasification _____

Only *gassed* and *gassing* follow the doubling principle—
other forms are exceptions.

In the case of *bus*, you may double the *s* or not, as you
choose, before adding *-es*.

Either buses _____

or busses _____

(Neither is the preferable form, though *buses* is seen
more frequently and is the only spelling used by the
New York Times. *Bus* is a shortened form of *omnibus*,
and so it is not originally a one-syllable word—and the
location of the accent in *omnibus* is, as you will learn
in a later chapter, the factor which influences the single
s.)

However, *bussed* and *bussing* (that is, using a *bus*, not
forms of *buss*, to kiss) are the usual spellings.

So we might conclude with a final point.

Point 30

In *gases*, *gaseous*, *gasify*, etc., the final *s* of *gas* is not doubled, though in *gassed* and *gassing* it is. Either *buses* or *busses* is acceptable.

This chapter has given you the essential preparation you need for harder and more important work ahead— work that deals with the complex concept of *accent*. Before getting into any more trouble, however, test your understanding of what we have already discussed.

TEST YOURSELF

I. Add the indicated suffix to the following words, then rewrite.

1. blur + -*ed* _____ (blurred)
2. rob + -*ed* _____ (robbed)
3. can + -*ing* _____ (canning)
4. run + -*er* _____ (runner)
5. sob + -*ing* _____ (sobbing)
6. thin + -*er* _____ (thinner)
7. thin + -*ness* _____ (thinness)
8. quiz + -*es* _____ (quizzes)
9. quiz + -*ed* _____ (quizzed)
10. quiz + -*ing* _____ (quizzing)
11. quiz + -*ical* _____ (quizzical)
12. gas + -*es* _____ (gases)
13. gas + -*ed* _____ (gassed)
14. gas + -*ing* _____ (gassing)
15. gas + -*eous* _____ (gaseous)
16. gas + -*ify* _____ (gasify)
17. ship + -*ing* _____ (shipping)
18. ship + -*ment* _____ (shipment)
19. twit + -*ed* _____ (twitted)
20. scar + -*ed* _____ (scarred)
21. lap + -*ing* _____ (lapping)
22. skin + -*er* _____ (skinner)

23. drum + -ed _____ (drummed)
24. drum + -ful _____ (drumful)
25. bus + -es _____ (buses or busses)

21 *(Thirteenth Day, continued)*

When to Double a *t*

PROBLEM

alloted *or* allotted?
benefited *or* benefitted?

SOLUTION

We have learned, then, under Point 29, that:
In a one-syllable word which ends in a *single consonant*—
Preceded by a *single vowel*—
The final consonant is doubled before adding a suffix—
If that suffix starts with a *vowel.*
As applied to one-syllable words, that is as much of the doubling principle as you have to know.

But since most spelling problems occur when suffixes are added to two- and three-syllable words (usually verbs), there are further ramifications and qualifications of the doubling principle with which you will wish to become thoroughly and comfortably familiar.

Purely for the sake of simplicity, let us concentrate, in this chapter, on words of two or three syllables which end in the letter *t*—but bear in mind that anything you learn will apply with equal force to all similar words no matter what the final consonant.

Our doubling principle still applies only to *words which end in a single consonant preceded by a single vowel.* Consider these special examples:

GROUP I

to acquit	to allot
to commit	to regret
to abet	to abut
to forget	to admit
to beset	to transmit

In addition to the common ending (the final single consonant, preceded by a single vowel), these words have another common characteristic.

All of them are accented on the last syllable.

We say:

ac-QUIT	al-LOT
com-MIT	re-GRET
a-BET	a-BUT
for-GET	ad-MIT
be-SET	trans-MIT

Such words are different, in this important particular, from the following examples, which are *not accented on the last syllable.*

GROUP II

to banquet—*BANG-quet*
to covet—*KUV-et*
to benefit—*BEN-e-fit*
to merit—*MER-it*
to profit—*PROF-it*
to prohibit—*pro-HIB-it*
to inhibit—*in-HIB-it*
to discomfit—*diss-KUM-fit*
to rivet—*RIV-et*
to visit—*VIZ-it*

This point of difference is most crucial. Though both sets of words end in a single consonant preceded by a single vowel—

One set is accented on the final syllable (Group I).

The other set is accented *on some syllable other than the final one* (Group II).

And the doubling principle applies, in the case of two- or three-syllable words, *only to those accented on the final syllable.*

That is, only to words of the type illustrated in Group I.

So—

Let us now add suffixes to the words in Group I, remembering—

That we double the final consonant if—

1. The word ends in a *single consonant*
2. Preceded by a *single vowel*
3. And is accented *on the final syllable*
4. And, moreover, the suffix to be added starts with a *vowel*.

These are, as you will recall, the same conditions required, as we discussed them in Chapter 20, for doubling in one-syllable words—*with the important addition of final syllable accent.*

DOUBLE THE FINAL CONSONANT

acquit' + -ing = acqui**tt**ing _____
commit' + -ed = commi**tt**ed _____
abet' + -ing = abe**tt**ing _____
(un)forget' + -able = unforge**tt**able _____
beset' + -ing = bese**tt**ing _____
allot' + -ed = allo**tt**ed _____
regret' + -able = regre**tt**able _____
abut' + -ed = abu**tt**ed _____
admit' + -ance = admi**tt**ance _____
transmit' + -al = transmi**tt**al _____

If we add a suffix beginning with a *consonant*, we do not, of course, double.

DO NOT DOUBLE THE FINAL CONSONANT

commit' + -ment = commitment _____

allot' + -ment = allotment _____

regret' + -ful - regretful _____

abut' + -ment = abutment _____

And if the word is of the type in Group II, with the accent _on other than the final syllable_, we again do not double.

DO NOT DOUBLE THE FINAL CONSONANT

ban'quet + -ing = banqueting _____

cov'et + -ous = covetous _____

ben'efit + -ed = benefited _____

mer'it + -ing - meriting _____

prof'it -ing - profiting _____

prohib'it + -ed = prohibited _____

inhib'it + -ing - inhibiting _____

discom'fit + -ing - discomfiting _____

riv'et + -er = riveter _____

vis'it + -ed = visited _____

Well, how does it look so far?

The doubling principle is gradually becoming more and more elaborate—but with the preparation you have had it should no longer sound too complicated.

We still do not have the entire formula for doubling final consonants—but let us gather what items we are now familiar with into a basic principle:

Point 31

If a word of more than one syllable—

Ends in a _single consonant_—
   (permit)

Preceded by a _single vowel_—
   (permit)

And receives the accent _on the last syllable_—
   (per-mit')

Double the final consonant—

When adding a suffix that starts with a *vowel*.
  (per-mit' + -ed = permitted)

No special cases?

But of course—there almost always are special cases.

Take *ricochet* and *crochet*.

Ricochet and *crochet* satisfy all the requirements of the doubling principle.

They both end in single consonants preceded by single vowels—

And the accent is on the last syllable.

But their pronunciation is unusual—the final *t* is silent:

> ricochet—*rick-o-SHAY*
> crochet—*cro-SHAY*

Both words are directly derived from French, in which interesting language *-et* is pronounced *ay*.

And in both words, or any similar ones in which final *-et* is pronounced *ay*, *we do not double the t before a suffix.*

    ricochet + -ing = ricocheting _____
    ricochet + -ed = ricocheted _____
    crochet + -ing = crocheting _____
    crochet + -ed = crocheted _____
    crochet + -er = crocheter _____

These words are pronounced:

> ricocheting—*rick-o-SHAY-ing*
> ricocheted—*rick-o-SHAYD*
> *crocheting—cro-SHAY-ing*
> crocheted—*cro-SHAYD*
> crocheter—*cro-SHAY-er*

We can thus add a new principle:

Point 32

If final *t* is silent, as in *ricochet* and *crochet*, do not double the final consonant when adding a suffix.

Or take, as another very special case, to *outfit*.

Outfit, as a verb, is pronounced *OUT-fit*, with the accent on the first syllable.

It thus violates one of the requirements of the doubling principle, even though it satisfies all the others.

Nevertheless, the *t* is doubled before a suffix beginning with a vowel.

outfitting _____
outfitted _____
outfitter _____

The reason is fairly obvious.

Actually, this is the verb *fit* plus a special prefix.

So we operate under the principle that applies to one-syllable words, disregarding the position of the accent.

Similar words offer no problem, since the accent falls on the last syllable.

For example:

out-RUN'—outrunning, etc.
out-SIT'—outsitting, etc.
un-FIT'—unfitted, etc.
be-FIT'—befitting, etc.

In the class of *out' fit* is a word like *wood' cut*, in which the accent is on *wood*. In actuality, however, we are dealing with the one-syllable verb *cut*, and so we disregard accent and write *woodcutter*, having doubled the final *t*.

That does it, so far.

We have added the concept of *accent* to the many other requirements of the doubling principle—and there is still one more qualification to learn.

This qualification will be discussed in Chapter 22, when we consider the concept of "accent shift." Eventually you will understand the doubling principle in all its multifarious aspects, with all its complicated qualifications and exceptions, with all its elaborate conditions.

Within a short time, you will have the doubling principle under such full control that you will automatically double or refrain from doubling without even thinking of the rule.

For note this about rules.

Rules, like mnemonics, are a means, not an end.

No one will ever ask you to quote a rule word for word—

And you have not, I hope, been making any attempt to memorize rules verbatim.

If you can quote the rule but you still misspell the word to which the rule applies, then, obviously your approach is all wrong.

You are trying to learn rules instead of learning to spell.

Like a mnemonic, a rule has only one purpose—

And that is to *explain* a spelling, so that you can adjust intellectually to the correct pattern of letters and thus become visually and kinesthetically accustomed to it.

So that you can become so accustomed to the correct pattern that the rule fades from your conscious mind, but the unconscious visual and kinesthetic memories remain forever.

Learn spelling rules, and especially the complex doubling principle, not as a memory feat, but solely as a means of adjusting to the correct patterns of large groups of words.

In short, *understand* the rule and how it applies—

Do not attempt to memorize it.

TEST YOURSELF

Add the indicated suffix to each word. Note where the accent falls in each case before you decide whether or not to double the final consonant—and notice also whether the suffix to be added starts with a vowel or consonant.

When to Double a *t*

1. ac-quit' + -*ed* _____ (acquitted)
2. ac-quit' + -*al* _____ (acquittal)
3. com-mit' + -*ed* _____ (committed)
4. com-mit' + -*ment* _____ (commitment)
5. ben'-efit + -*ed* _____ (benefited)
6. ben'-efit + -*ing* _____ (benefiting)
7. val'-et + -*ed* _____ (valeted)
8. a-bet' + -*ed* _____ (abetted)
9. for-get' + -*ing* _____ (forgetting)
10. al-lot' + -*ed* _____ (allotted)
11. al-lot' + -*ment* _____ (allotment)
12. re-gret' + -*ed* _____ (regretted)
13. a-but' + -*ment* _____ (abutment)
14. ad-mit' + -*ing* _____ (admitting)
15. trans-mit' + -*ed* _____ (transmitted)
16. cov'-et + -*ing* _____ (coveting)
17. prof'-it + -*er* _____ (profiter)
18. com-mit' + -*ee* _____ (committee)
19. cor'-set + -*ed* _____ (corseted)
20. be-fit' + -*ing* _____ (befitting)
21. o-mit' + -*ed* _____ (omitted)
22. outwit' + -*ed* _____ (outwitted)
23. mis-be-got' + -*en* _____ (misbegotten)
24. wood'-cut + -*er* _____ (woodcutter)
25. mer'-it + -*ed* _____ (merited)
26. re-gret' + -*ful* _____ (regretful)
27. dis-com'-fit + -*ure* _____ (discomfiture)
28. in-hib'-it + -*ion* _____ (inhibition)
29. riv'-et + -*ed* _____ (riveted)
30. sub-mit' + -*ed* _____ (submitted)
31. un-fit' + -*ed* _____ (unfitted)
32. in-ter-mit' + -*ent* _____ (intermittent)
33. vis'-it + *or* _____ (visitor)
34. cro-chet' + -*ing* _____ (crocheting)
35. cro-chet' + -*ed* _____ (crocheted)

36. ri-co-chet' + -ed _____ (ricocheted)
37. ri-co-chet' + ing _____ (ricocheting)
38. prof'-it + -ed _____ (profited)
39. in-hib'-it + -ed _____ (inhibited)
40. pro-hib'-it + -ion _____ (prohibition)
41. per-mit' + -er _____ (permitter)
42. per-mit' + -ed _____ (permitted)
43. per-mit' + -ing _____ (permitting)
44. dis-com'-fit + -ed _____ (discomfited)
45. trans-mit' + -al _____ (transmittal)
46. riv'-et + -er _____ (riveter)

How a Shifting Accent May Alter the Spelling

PROBLEM

occurence *or* occurrence?
deference *or* deferrence?
occuring *or* occurring?
defering *or* deferring?

SOLUTION

To complete our total understanding of the doubling principle, we wish to explore in this chapter words which end in the single consonant *r*—

Because in such words, almost exclusively, there enters the new factor of *accent shift*.

And *accent shift* will exercise an important influence on your decision to double a consonant or leave it alone.

Accent shift sounds like a scholarly and academic phrase—it is actually, however, quite easy to understand.

Let me illustrate.

Take *prefer*.

You will recognize it at once as a word that meets all the requirements so far detailed for the operation of the doubling principle.

Prefer ends in a single consonant (*r*) preceded by a single vowel (*e*).

Prefer is accented on the last syllable *(pre-FER')*.

If you decided to add a suffix which starts with a vowel (*-ed, -ing*, etc.) you would expect to double the *r*, producing *preferred, preferring*, etc.

And you would, of course, be absolutely right in doubling the *r*.

Note, now, that *prefer* has two syllables: *pre-fer'*.

The accent falls on the last syllable, on the *-fer*.

In *preferred* and *preferring*, the accent remains on the same syllable on which it fell in *pre-FER'*; *pre-FERD'*, *pre-FER'*-ing.

There has been no accent shift.

But suppose we add the ending *-ence* to *prefer*?

Do we double the *r* or leave it alone?

Or suppose we add the ending *-able* or *-ential* to *prefer*?

Again, do we double the *r* or leave it alone?

As it happens, in these cases we leave it alone.

Point 33

When the accent *shifts* as a result of adding a suffix to a verb, you do not double the final consonant.

Note in the chart below how often *accent shift* occurs in verbs which end in a single *r* preceded by a single vowel. And in every instance in which such *accent shift* occurs, we do *not* double the *r*.

CHART 1

Original Verb	*Form with Added Suffix*
(Single final consonant preceded by single vowel, accent on last syllable)	(Note that the accent shifts and the original final consonant is not doubled)
(in-FER') infer	*(IN'-fer-ence)* inference _____
	(in-fer-EN'-sh'l) inferential _____
(re-FER') refer	*(REF'-er-ence)* reference _____
	(REF'-er-EE') referee _____

CHART 1 (*continued*)

Original Verb	*Form with Added Suffix*
	(*REF'-er-EN'-dum*) referendum __
	(*REF'-er-ent*) referent _____
(*con-FER'*) confer	(*CON'-fer-ence*) conference _____
	(*CON'-fer-EE'*) conferee _____
(*de-FER'*) defer	(*DEF'-er-ence*) deference _____
	(*def-er-EN'-sh'l*) deferential _____
(*pre-FER'*) prefer	(*PREF'-er-ence*) preference _____
	(*PREF'-er-a-b'l*) preferable _____
	(*pref-er-EN'-sh'l*) preferential ___

The foregoing chart merits a few moments of careful study. As soon as you see what I'm driving at, you will understand the final factor in the doubling principle—namely, *that the accent must REMAIN on the original final syllable before you double that original final consonant.*

To make this factor even clearer, let me chart these same verbs in combination with their forms which require the doubled consonant—the forms, that is, in which the accent does *not* shift.

CHART II

Original Verb	Form With Added Suffix
(Accent on last syllable)	(No shift in accent)
(*in-FER'*) infer	(*in-FERD'*) inferred _____
	(*in-FER'-ing*) inferring _____
(*re-FER'*) refer	(*re-FERD'*) referred _____
	(*re-FER'-ing*) referring _____
(*con-FER'*) confer	(*con-FERD'*) conferred _____
	(*con-FER'-ing*) conferring _____
(*de-FER'*) defer	(*de-FERD'*) deferred _____
	(*de-FER'-ing*) deferring _____
(*pre-FER'*) prefer	(*pre-FERD'*) preferred _____
	(*pre-FER'-ing*) preferring _____

A little study will clearly show the contrast between the two charts.

In Chart I, the accent shifts when the suffix is added, *and the r is not doubled.*

In Chart II, the accent does *not* shift, i.e., it remains on the original last syllable, *and the r is doubled.*

Charts of course always look a little forbidding.

Don't let these two charts frighten you—they're simple to understand and contain the key to an important factor of the doubling principle.

Let me emphasize this factor by repeating—

Point 33

If a word complies with all other qualifications of the doubling principle, *but suffers a shift in accent when a suffix is added, the original final consonant is not doubled.*

That isn't too difficult—and with all the work you have devoted to analyzing, understanding, and becoming adjusted to the various factors of the doubling principle, you are ready now to see the total principle in all its explicit wording without getting lost in the somewhat complex phraseology.

THE TOTAL DOUBLING PRINCIPLE

Condition 1

If a word contains a single syllable and ends in *a single consonant* preceded by *a single vowel*—

(h**op**)

Condition 2

Or if it contains two or more syllables; ends in a single consonant preceded by a single vowel; *and is accented on the final syllable*—

(comm**it**′, but *not* cov′**et**)

You double the final consonant before adding a suffix—

Condition 3

If the suffix begins with a vowel—

(ho**pp**ing, commi**tt**ing, but coveting, commitment)

Condition 4

Provided the accent does *not* shift off the original final syllable.

(occur'—occur'rence; but prefer'—pref'erence)

And that's it—taking care of all possible variations and omitting, so far, only a few isolated exceptional cases, which, of course, need always to be reckoned with.

These isolated exceptional cases will be considered in a later chapter. But first the usual test of your learning.

TEST YOURSELF

Add the indicated suffix to each verb, remaining alert to whether the accent does or does not shift when the longer form is complete, and realizing, as always, that the doubling principle operates only if the suffix starts with a vowel.

1. infer' + -*ed* _____ (infe**rr**ed)
2. prefer' + -*ing* _____ (prefe**rr**ing)
3. prefer' + -*ence* _____ (prefe**r**ence)
4. prefer' + -*ential* _____ (prefe**r**ential)
5. prefer' + -*ment* _____ (prefe**r**ment)
6. infer' + -*ence* _____ (infe**r**ence)
7. refer' + -*ed* _____ (refe**rr**ed)
8. refer' + -*ence* _____ (refe**r**ence)
9. refer' + -*ent* _____ (refe**r**ent)
10. confer' + -*ing* _____ (confe**rr**ing)
11. confer' + -*ence* _____ (confe**r**ence)
12. confer' + -*ee* _____ (confe**r**ee)
13. aver' + -*ed* _____ (ave**rr**ed)
14. bestir' + -*ing* _____ (besti**rr**ing)

15. defer' + -ment _____ (deferment)
16. defer' + -ence _____ (deference)
17. defer' + -ing _____ (deferring)
18. deter' + -ent _____ (deterrent)
19. deter' + -ence _____ (deterrence)
20. deter' + -ed _____ (deterred)
21. demur' + -al _____ (demurral)
22. demur' + -ed _____ (demurred)
23. incur' + -ence _____ (incurrence)
24. incur' + -ing _____ (incurring)
25. occur' + -ence _____ (occurrence)
26. occur' + -ing _____ (occurring)
27. recur' + -ence _____ (recurrence)
28. befur' + -ed _____ (befurred)
29. concur' + -ence _____ (concurrence)
30. inter' + -ed _____ (interred)
31. inter' + -ment _____ (interment)
32. occur' + -ed _____ (occurred)

A Quick New Look at the Doubling Principle

PROBLEMS

kidnaped *or* kidnapped?
counselor *or* counsellor?
development *or* developement?
developed *or* developped?

SOLUTION

We have covered now, with detailed thoroughness and in almost all possible contingencies, the principles that govern the doubling of final consonants when suffixes are added.

We explored, in Chapter 20, one-syllable words to which the doubling principle applies, and you learned:

—That if such words end in a single consonant preceded by a single vowel, you double that consonant before adding a suffix beginning with a vowel: bag—baggage, strip—stripping, etc.

—That important exceptional cases are gases, gaseous, gasify, etc., and the optional spelling buses.

In Chapter 21 we considered words of more than one syllable, and you learned:

—To be alert to the position of the accent, doubling when the accent falls on the final syllable (al-lot′—allott'-ed, per-mit'—per-mitt'ing, etc.), but not when the accent falls on any other syllable (ben'e-fit—ben'e-fit -ing, prof'-it—prof'-it-ed, etc.).

We discussed, in Chapter 22, the influence of accent shifts, and you learned:

—To refrain from doubling if the accent *shifts off* the original final syllable (pre-fer'—pref'-er-ence, de-fer'— def-er-en'tial).

—To double in the same words if the accent *does not* shift (pre-fer'—pre-ferred', de-fer'—de-ferr'ing, occur'— occurr'ence, etc.).

And now, because the doubling principle is the most complicated of all the rules of English spelling, but also one of the most valuable, far-reaching, and trustworthy, it will pay us to take a quick run-down on it, highlighting, for purposes of productive review, words of more than one syllable ending in consonants other than the two (namely *t* and *r*) on which we concentrated in previous pages.

I

We know that we double the final consonant of a word before adding a vowel suffix provided:

The original verb ended in a single consonant preceded by a single vowel—

The accent falls on the last syllable—

And the accent does not shift off that original last syllable in the longer form.

For example:

    1. equip—equipped _____
             equipping _____
    2. reship—reshipping _____
             reshipped _____
    3. begin—beginning _____
             beginner _____

4. control—controlled _____
               controlling _____
               controller _____
5. rebel—rebellious _____
            rebellion _____
            rebelled _____
            rebelling _____
6. excel—excelled _____
            excelling _____
7. patrol—patrolled _____
            patrolling _____
8. annul—annulled _____
            annulling _____
9. compel—compelling _____
            compelled _____
10. propel—propelling _____
            propelled _____

II

On the other hand, we know that we do not double the final consonant of words in which the accent falls on *other than the last syllable*. For example:

1. mur'mur—murmured, etc. _____
2. of'fer—offering, etc. _____
3. devel'op—devel'oping _____
              devel'oped _____
              devel'oper _____
4. gal'lop—gal'loping _____
             gal'loped _____
             gal'loper _____
5. wor'ship—wor'shiped _____
             wor'shiping _____
             wor'shiper _____
6. envel'op—envel'oped _____
             envel'oping _____

7. kid'nap—kid'naping _____

    kid'naped _____

    kid'naper _____

(Note the one *p* in all forms of *kidnap*. The double *p* in the longer forms is conventional British practice and occasionally found in American usage—but the regular single *p* form is preferred.)

8. impris'on—impris'oned, etc. _____

9. liv'en—livening, etc. _____

10. trav'el—trave'eler _____

    trav'eling _____

    trav'eled _____

11. can'cel—canceled _____

    can'celing _____

    can'celable _____

    can'celer _____

12. coun'sel—counseling _____

    coun'seled _____

    coun'selor _____

13. coun'cil—coun'cilor _____

14. sig'nal—sig'naling _____

    sig'naled _____

    sig'naler _____

15. shov'el—shov'eled _____

    shov'eler _____

    shov'eling _____

16. mar'vel—mar'velous _____

    mar'veled, etc. _____

(In examples 10–16, and in most other similar words ending in *l* and accented on the first syllable, the double *l* in the longer form is conventional British usage, and occasionally found in American writing. The single *l* form, however, is preferable and safer in this type of word.)

III

Let us now take, for the sake of complete clarity, overlearning, and thorough review, a final group of words which adhere to one of the qualifications of the doubling principle.

In the following forms the final consonant *is not doubled* because the suffix added starts with a *consonant*, not with a vowel.

1. equip + -ment = equipment _____
2. reship + -ment = reshipment _____
3. patrol + -man = patrolman _____
4. annul + -ment = annulment _____
5. develop + -ment = development _____
6. envelop + -ment = envelopment _____
7. worship + -ful = worshipful _____

(*Develop, envelop,* and *worship* would not double the *p* in any case, of course, since the accent does not fall on the last syllable—and the consonant at the beginning of the suffix is a kind of double insurance. Note that there is no *e* after the *p* in *development* or *envelopment*, though the use of the unnecessary *e* is a common and prevalent error. The verbs end in *p* and *-ment* is added—no need for inserting the *e.*)

If you fully understand the three charts around which this chapter is built, you are a master of the doubling principle. You can now make an immediate and accurate decision as to whether to double a final consonant or leave it alone—and you can make that decision with full assurance that you know both what you're doing and why you're doing it.

Unless, of course, you are dealing with an exceptional case.

We'll consider the important exceptions in the next chapter—but first, as usual,

---

TEST YOURSELF

Rewrite each word by adding the indicated suffix to the verb, remaining alert to the position of the accent and to whether the suffix starts with a vowel or consonant. Use, in all cases, the preferred American form.

I. Add -ed

1. equip' _____ (equipped)
2. control' _____ (controlled)
3. rebel' _____ (rebelled)
4. excel' _____ (excelled)
5. patrol' _____ (patrolled)
6. annul' _____ (annulled)
7. compel' _____ (compelled)
8. propel' _____ (propelled)
9. repel' _____ (repelled)
10. impel' _____ (impelled)
11. expel' _____ (expelled)
12. dispel' _____ (dispelled)
13. of'fer _____ (offered)
14. devel'op _____ (developed)
15. gal'lop _____ (galloped)

II: Add -ing:

1. equip' _____ (equipping)
2. begin' _____ (beginning)
3. control' _____ (controlling)
4. rebel' _____ (rebelling)
5. excel' _____ (excelling)
6. patrol' _____ (patrolling)
7. annul' _____ (annulling)
8. compel' _____ (compelling)
9. repel' _____ (repelling)
10. impel' _____ (impelling)
11. expel' _____ (expelling)

12. dispel' _____ (dispelling)
13. dif'fer _____ (differing)
14. gal'lop _____ (galloping)
15. devel'op _____ (developing)
16. wal'lop _____ (walloping)
17. envel'op _____ (enveloping)
18. wor'ship _____ (worshiping)
19. kid'nap _____ (kidnaping)
20. rav'el _____ (raveling)

III. Add -er or -or:

1. begin' _____ (beginner)
2. control' _____ (controller)
3. expel' _____ (expeller)
4. of'fer _____ (offerer)
5. devel'op _____ (developer)
6. wor'ship _____ (worshiper)
7. kid'nap _____ (kidnaper)
8. trav'el _____ (traveler)
9. coun'sel _____ (counselor)
10. coun'cil _____ (councilor)
11. sig'nal _____ (signaler)
12. jew'el _____ (jeweler)
13. grov'el _____ (groveler)
14. mod'el _____ (modeler)
15. shov'el _____ (shoveler)

IV. Add -ment:

1. equip _____ (equipment)
2. reship _____ (reshipment)
3. annul _____ (annulment)
4. develop _____ (development)
5. envelop _____ (envelopment)

A Footnote on Controller-Comptroller
If you have ever been intrigued, and possibly a little puzzled, by the spelling *comptroller*, you may be inter-

ested to learn that this pattern is now obsolete except as the title of the treasurer of a corporation or of a government organization; in which areas of American life adherence to tradition is sometimes so strong that modern usage has a hard time. It may very well be that *comptroller* seems more impressive and dignified than *controller*, but both words are pronounced identically (*kon-TROL-er*) and there is no rational need for the ancient and illogical spelling.

MNEMONICS

(Fourteenth Day, continued) **Eight**

PRETEST

1. pro**noun**ciation *or* pro**nun**ciation?
2. sacr**i**legious *or* sacr**e**ligious?
3. gene**o**logy *or* gene**a**logy?
4. miner**o**logy *or* miner**a**logy?
5. main**tain**ance *or* main**ten**ance?

MNEMONICS

One thing you *cannot* bank on in English spelling: that if you can pronounce a word you can also spell it—correctly.

Spelling often enough follows pronunciation—just as often, especially in the troublesome words, it does not.

Take *victuals*—pronounced, of all things, *vittles*. Or *viscount*, pronounced *VYE-kount*. Or *phlegmatic*, in which the *g* is sounded, and *phlegm*, in which it is silent. Or *column*, in which the *n* is silent, and *columnist*, in which it is sounded.

Or, of course, the famous *-ough* combinations—

> pronounced OFF, in *cough*
> pronounced OO, in *through*
> pronounced O, in *though*
> pronounced OU, in *bough*
> pronounced UFF, in *rough*

And so on, without end.

However, there are a number of demons which *can* be spelled correctly if pronounced carefully. Five such demons are the words in the pretest of this chapter—all of which have the common mnemonic of careful pronunciation.

1. (pro**noun**ciation *or* pro**nun**ciation?)

Be alert when you come to the second syllable of this word—which is pronounced and spelled *nun*.

> *Correct Spelling:* pro**nun**ciation _____
> *Mnemonic:* pro-**NUN**-ci-a-tion

2. (sacri**le**geous *or* sacre**li**gious?)

In the preferable form of this word, the second syllable is pronounced *ri* (as in *rim*), the following syllable *ee* (as in *legal*); suiting spelling to sound, we write SAC-RI-LE-GIOUS. Do not confuse SACR**I**LEGIOUS with *religious*; the two words are sharply dissimilar in meaning and have an opposite combination of the vowels *i* and *e*.

The noun from SACRILEGIOUS has the pattern you would expect: SACR**I**LEGE.

> *Correct Spelling:* sacr**i**legious _____
> *Mnemonic:* sac-**ri**-LE-gious

3. (gene**o**logy *or* gene**a**logy?)

Most such words (and there are hundreds of them) do end in *-ology*—this is one of the three common ones which end in *-alogy*. Pronounce and spell it ge-ne-**AL**-o-gy;

> *Correct Spelling:* gene**a**logy _____
> *Mnemonic:* ge-ne-**AL**-o-gy

4. (miner**o**logy *or* miner**a**logy?)

And MINER**A**LOGY is the second of the three common words which end in *-alogy*. Pronounce and spell it min-er-**AL**-o-gy. (The third word is *analogy*, usually pronounced and spelled without error.) Note also that MINER**A**LOGY comes from MINER**A**L.

Correct Spelling: mineralogy _____
Mnemonic: min-er-**AL**-o-gy

5. (main**tain**ance *or* main**ten**ance?)

Although the verb is *maintain*, pronounced as spelled, the noun form changes *-tain* to *-ten*, and is pronounced accordingly: MAIN-**ten**-ance. This is similar, as you notice, to the change from PRO**NOUN**CE to PRO**NUN**-CIATION.

Correct Spelling: main**ten**ance _____
Mnemonic: MAIN-**ten**-ance

MNEMONICS CHART

1. pro**nun**ciation _____   pro-**NUN**ci-a-tion
2. sac**ri**legious _____   sac-ri-**LE**-gious
3. gene**al**ogy _____   ge-ne-**AL**-o-gy
4. miner**al**ogy _____   min-er-**AL**-o-gy
5. main**ten**ance _____   MAIN-**ten**-ance

TEST YOURSELF

I. Check the correct pattern.
1. (a) minerology,   (b) mineralogy   (b)
2. (a) sacrilegious,   (b) sacreligious   (a)
3. (a) pronounciation,   (b) pronunciation   (b)
4. (a) maintenance,   (b) maintainance   (a)
5. (a) geneology,   (b) genealogy   (b)

II. Recall the mnemonic for each word.
1. accelerate _____   (celerity)
2. occurrence _____   (current event)
3. anoint _____   (an oil)
4. devise _____   (devious)
5. superintendent _____   (rent)
6. iridescent _____   (iris)
7. inoculate _____   (inject)

   8. tranquillity _____ **(quill)**
   9. grammar _____ **(mar)**
10. indispensable _____ **(able** worker)

III. Decide on the crucial missing letter or letters, then rewrite the complete word.

   1. miner—logy _____ (a)
   2. maint—nance _____ (e)
   3. pron—nciation _____ (u)
   4. sacr—l—gious _____ (i,e)
   5. gene—logy _____ (a)
   6. i—o—ulate _____ (n,c)
   7. indispens—ble _____ (a)
   8. superintend—nt _____ (e)
   9. tranqui—ity _____ (ll)
10. i—idescent _____ (r)
11. gramm—r _____ (a)
12. occu—nce _____ (rre)
13. d—vise _____ (e)
14. acce—erate _____ (l)
15. a—oint _____ (n)

How to Handle Real and Apparent Violations of the Doubling Principle

PROBLEMS

combating *or* combatting?
crystalize *or* crystallize?
canvases *or* canvasses?
chagrined *or* chagrinned?

SOLUTION

Now that you are a master of the doubling principle—
Now that you are familiar and at ease with all its complex provisions—
Now that you can handle, without hesitation, every *regular* doubling problem that can possibly occur—
You are ready to study some of the *irregular* problems, those plaguing and perplexing exceptional cases which are likely to cause confusion.

These exceptional cases, in most instances, have neither rhyme nor reason (but where any helpful reasons exist, I'll pass them along to you), and you will simply have to accept them as rebels or misfits, relying strongly on your visual memory and on the fact that exceptions somehow manage to stick in the mind with no great effort. These are blocks that we can't comfortably fit into the general structure of the doubling principle—so we'll let them stand out conspicuously.

Exceptional Case 1

Can'cel, chan'cel, crys'tal, met'al, and tran'quil are, as you can see, accented on the first syllable rather than the last syllable. By the provisions of the doubling principle, therefore, we should not double the final consonant before adding a vowel suffix—*canceled, canceling, metaled,* etc.

Nevertheless, in the following, and only the following, *exceptional forms*, we *do* double the final *l*. These are exceptions to the doubling principle and should be learned as such.

1. cancellation _____
2. chancellery _____
3. chancellor _____
4. crystallize _____
5. crystalline _____
6. metallic _____
7. metallurgy _____
8. tranquillity _____

Exceptional Case 2

Excel is accented on the last syllable—hence we write *excelled* and *excelling*. In *excellent* and *excellence* the accent shifts and, by a provision of the doubling principle, only one *l* should be required. Nevertheless, the only correct forms contain double *l*'s.

9. excellent _____
10. excellence _____

Exceptional Case 3

Chagrin (pronounced *sha-GRIN*) is accented on the last syllable—we should therefore double final *n* before adding a vowel suffix. But we don't. The only correct patterns, strange as they may look, are:

1. chagrining _____
12. chagrined _____

Exceptional Case 4

Handicap is accented on the first syllable—by the doubling principle we would not expect to double the final *p*. However, we do.

13. handicapping _____
14. handicapped _____
15. handicapper _____

The reason for this anomaly is the fact that the word is a combination of *cap* plus *handy*—and we treat it as a one-syllable verb, following the analogy of *capping, capper*, etc. We react similarly to other verbs which are made up of two words, even though the accent does not occur on the last syllable—for example *horse'-whip, o'verstep, weath'erstrip, eaves'drop, o'vertip*, etc.

Thus:

16. horsewhi**pp**ed, _____   19. eavesdro**pp**ing, _____
    etc.   etc.
17. overste**pp**ing _____   20. overti**pp**er, _____
    etc.   etc.
18. weatherstri**pp**ed, ____
    etc.

And we have the same reaction also to *hum'bug* and *zig'zag*. Accent is on the first syllable, but we are influenced by the words *bug* and *zag*, and so we write only:

21. humbu**gg**ed _____   23. zigza**gg**ed _____
22. humbu**gg**ing _____   24. zigza**gg**ing _____

(Apparently) Exceptional Case 5

Bias and *focus* (pronounced *BYE-'ss, FO-k'ss*) are accented on the first rather than the last syllable. By the doubling principle, therefore, we should *not* double final *s*, and you will be happy to hear that in America it is preferred usage not to.

25. biases _____   28. focuses _____
26. biased _____   29. focused _____
27. biasing _____   30. focusing _____

You may therefore be confused by these correct spellings:

31. canvasses _____   33. canvassing _____
32. canvassed _____   34. canvasser _____

Especially when you know that the accent in each instance is on the first syllable only.

As soon as you realize the parent verb from which forms 31–34 come, your confusion will vanish. The original verb is *canvass*, not *canvas*. Note the double *s* in the original verb and you will understand the double *s* in the longer, derived forms. *Canvass*, ending not in a single consonant but in double *s*, does not operate under the doubling principle.

But what about *canvas*?

Canvas (one *s*) is a noun only, meaning either a kind of cloth or a painting. It has a plural *canvases*, but should not be confused with the verb to *canvass*, which in all forms contains the double *s*.

(Apparently) Exceptional Case 6

The verb *to combat* may cause considerable confusion.

Originally (and up to about ten years ago) practically the only pronunciation heard from educated speakers was COM′bat, accent on the first syllable.

But, especially lately, the verb has been receiving a second-syllable accent (com-BAT′), not only on the popular level but also from large groups of cultivated speakers— and is thus sanctioned by modern dictionaries.

Which makes for a dilemma.

Do we suit the spelling of the longer forms of *combat* to the original, or to the newer and increasingly popular, pronunciation?

That is, do we double the *t* when we add the suffixes *-ed*, *-er*, *-ive*, *-ant*, and *-ing*, as we do in other verbs like *per-MIT′*, *com-MIT′*, etc., that are accented on the last syllable?

Or do we leave the *t* alone?

You will find the answer in this principle of English spelling:

Words rarely change their spelling no matter how radically the pronunciation changes.

So pronounce *combat* and its various forms in whatever way you like, with the accent either on the *com-* or on the *-bat*—but spell it as if the accent were always on the first syllable.

How to Handle Violations of the Doubling Principle

Thus:

35. combated _____
36. combating _____
37. combatant _____

38. combater _____
39. combative _____

Never a double *t* in any form of *combat*, no matter what pronunciation you habitually use and feel comfortable with.

Our six exceptional (or apparently exceptional) cases drive the final nail into our construction of the complete doubling principle—all possible aspects and important exceptions are now accounted for and hammered into place. No form of any verb can possibly be a matter of doubt once you completely understand every facet of, and exception to, this valuable principle.

Here, once again, are the thirty-nine words discussed in this chapter—become visually and kinesthetically familiar with them before you test your learning.

1. cancellation _____
2. chancellery _____
3. chancellor _____
4. crystallize _____
5. crystalline _____
6. metallic _____
7. metallurgy _____
8. tranquillity _____
9. excellent _____
10. excellence _____
11. chagrining _____
12. chagrined _____
13. handicapping _____
14. handicapped _____
15. handicapper _____
16. horsewhipped _____
17. overstepping _____

18. weatherstripped _____
19. eavesdropping _____
20. overtipper _____
21. humbugged _____
22. humbugging _____
23. zigzagged _____
24. zigzagging _____
25. biases _____
26. biased _____
27. biasing _____
28. focuses _____
29. focused _____
30. focusing _____
31. canvasses _____
32. canvassed _____
33. canvassing _____
34. canvasser _____

35. combated _____   38. combater _____
36. combating _____   39. combative _____
37. combatant _____

TEST YOURSELF

Rewrite the following words with the indicated suffix.

1. cancel + -*ation* _____   (cancellation)
2. excel + -*ency* _____   (excellency)
3. crystal + -*ize* _____   (crystallize)
4. metal + -*urgy* _____   (metallurgy)
5. tranquil + -*ity* _____   (tranquillity)
6. chagrin + -*ed* _____   (chagrined)
7. chagrin + -*ing* _____   (chagrining)
8. chancel + -*ery* _____   (chancellery)
9. chancel + -*or* _____   (chancellor)
10. crystal + -*ine* _____   (crystalline)
11. metal + -*ic* _____   (metallic)
12. handicap + -*ed* _____   (handicapped)
13. eavesdrop + -*ed* _____   (eavesdropped)
14. humbug + -*ed* _____   (humbugged)

A Note to the Overconscientious

You can make the acquisition of a high degree of skill in spelling a monotonous and needlessly difficult task—if you wish to.

You can accomplish this negative feat by strict and careful memorizing of the principles with which these pages deal, so that you can reel them off word by word.

If you manage finally to spout such verbatim reports of the spelling principles, you are learning rules, not spelling.

For spelling deals with individual words, not with general rules—and one facet of skill in spelling is an instantaneous and accurate reaction to a word by what we might call "successful grouping."

Which means that you recognize, from an *understanding*

of principles, that a word belongs in a certain category. For example, if called upon to write *analyze*, you recall it automatically as a member of the *analyze-paralyze* group, as one of the only two common words ending in *-yze*.

For example, if called upon to write *proceed*, you recall it automatically as one of the only three *-ceed* words in the language (*succeed, proceed, exceed*).

For example, if called upon to write *insistent*, you recall it automatically as one of the *rent* words—*insistent, persistent, superintendent, dependent*.

For example, if called upon to write *occurred*, you recall it automatically as one of the doubling words in which the accent remains on the original final syllable, a member of the *referred-preferred-incurred-inferred-* etc., group.

For example, if called upon to write *combated*, you recall it automatically as a form of one of the verbs in which the accent does not fall on the last syllable, despite its popular pronunciation. Or you recall *chagrined* as one of the exceptional cases under the doubling principle.

And so on.

Such ability to group a word successfully comes not from monotonously memorizing principles—

But rather, and most efficiently, from thoroughly *understanding* the provisions of, exceptions to, and where they exist, the reasons for, the principles that govern correct patterns.

Plus (and this is most important) constant *kinesthetic* and *visual* practice with all the individual words that occur under each principle.

As to this complicated and important doubling principle with which we have been working so carefully for the last few chapters—I beg you, make no attempt to memorize it to the point where you can repeat it verbatim.

Instead, bend your efforts to a full and active *understanding* of its provisions and exceptions. Become visually and kinesthetically adjusted to the individual words which the principle governs. And shortly, though the principle and all its complex phraseology may vanish from your conscious mind, there will be a residue of result which will make your spelling error-free on all words considered in these chapters.

In this way you will completely avoid the monotonous and needlessly difficult aspects of spelling—and become a perfect, or near-perfect, speller through active learning and stimulating experiences.

Third Review

Your training program is now three fourths complete—

And if you have been working intensively and conscientiously, you have developed to a high degree your visual and kinesthetic memory of the correct patterns of hundreds and hundreds of commonly misspelled words; you have made a healthy intellectual adjustment to a number of very important basic principles in English spelling.

Let us now review your grasp of the material in Chapters 18–24 and your ability to respond accurately with the proper patterns of the words discussed.

BASIC PRINCIPLES

1. The choice between *-cy* and *-sy*, or between *-ence* and *-ense*, will not be troublesome except in the following important words:

1. defense _____
2. offense _____
3. pretense _____
4. license _____
5. ecstasy _____

6. idiosyncrasy _____
7. apostasy _____
8. hypocrisy _____
9. to prophesy _____
   (the verb)

2. Similarly, in most words which allow a logical choice between *-ify* and *-efy*, the probable ending is *-ify*. But four words end in *-efy* only:

1. liquefy _____   3. stupefy _____
2. rarefy _____   4. putrefy _____

3. One-syllable words ending in a single consonant preceded by a single vowel double that final consonant before adding a vowel suffix:

(quiz) quizzes _____   (trip) (tripping _____
                          etc.

4. Exceptions are:

(gas) gases _____   (bus) buses _____
gaseous _____   (*busses* equally acceptable)
gasify _____   etc.

5. But *gassed* and *gassing* are not exceptions.

6. If a word contains more than one syllable, and the accent falls on the final syllable, with all other conditions of the doubling principle operating,[1] the final consonant is doubled—provided the addition of the suffix does not cause the accent to shift.

(allot) allotted _____   (commit) committed _____
                          etc.

7. But if the accent falls on any but the final syllable, the final consonant is *not* doubled:

(benefit) benefited _____   (profit) profiting _____
                          etc.

8. If a word ends in *-et* pronounced *ay*, the final consonant is *not* doubled when a suffix is added.

ricocheted _____   crocheted _____
                          etc.

---

[1]Single consonant preceded by a single vowel, suffix starting with a vowel.

9. Certain verbs made up of two separate parts are treated as one-syllable words—the final consonant is therefore doubled no matter where the accent falls.

outfitted _____   woodcutter _____
                            etc.

10. Even though a verb meets all the conditions of the doubling principle, if the addition of a suffix shifts the accent *off* the *original last syllable* the final consonant is *not* doubled. Most such examples end in *r*.

(defer) deference _____   (prefer) preference _____
                            etc.

11. The following important forms, among others (as explained in Chapter 24), are exceptional cases:

cancellation _____   chagrining _____
chancellery _____   chagrined _____
chancellor _____   handicapping _____
crystallize _____   canvassing _____
metallic _____   combated _____
metallurgy _____   combatant _____
tranquillity _____   combative _____
excellent _____   combating _____
excellence _____

THIRD REVIEW TEST

I. Add either *-cy* or *-sy*, to the following, rewriting the complete word.

    1. idiosyncra— _____ (sy)
    2. a prophe— _____ (cy)
       (noun)
    3. to prophe— _____ (sy)
       (verb)
    4. ecsta— _____ (sy)
    5. vacan— _____ (cy)

   6. pleuri— _____ (sy)
   7. courte— _____ (sy)
   8. pira— _____ (cy)
   9. aposta— _____ (sy)
  10. fanta— _____ (sy)
  11. suprema— _____ (cy)

II. Add either *-efy* or *-ify* to the following, rewriting the complete word.

   1. class— _____ (ify)
   2. liqu— _____ (efy)
   3. cert— _____ (ify)
   4. rar— _____ (efy)
   5. pac— _____ (ify)
   6. stup— _____ (efy)
   7. putr— _____ (efy)
   8. rat— _____ (ify)

III. Add the indicated ending to each word, rewriting in its complete form.

   1. gas + *-es* _____ (gases)
   2. bus + *-es* _____ (buses or
                                       (busses))
   3. gas + *-eous* _____ (gaseous)
   4. gas + *-ify* _____ (gasify)
   5. gas + *-ed* _____ (gassed)
   6. gas + *-ing* _____ (gassing)
   7. quiz + *-es* _____ (quizzes)
   8. quiz + *-ing* _____ (quizzing)
   9. quit + *-ing* _____ (quitting)
  10. ship + *-ing* _____ (shipping)
  11. ship + *-ment* _____ (shipment)
  12. scar + *-ed* _____ (scarred)
  13. begin + *-ing* _____ (beginning)
  14. allot + *-ed* _____ (allotted)
  15. allot + *-ment* _____ (allotment)
  16. benefit + *-ed* _____ (benefited)

17. acquit + -ed _____ (acquitted)
18. commit + -ing _____ (committing)
19. transmit + -al _____ (transmittal)
20. regret + -able _____ (regrettable)
21. banquet + -ed _____ (banqueted)
22. crochet + -ed _____ (crocheted)
23. occu + -ing _____ (occurring)
24. occur + -ence _____ (occurrence)
25. defer + -ing _____ (deferring)
26. defer + -ence _____ (deference)
27. refer + -ed _____ (referred)
28. refer + -ence _____ (reference)
29. deter + -ence _____ (deterrence)
30. abhor + -ent _____ (abhorrent)
31. concur + -ence _____ (concurrence)
32. demur + -al _____ (demurral)
33. kidnap + -er _____ (kidnaper)
34. counsel + -ed _____ (counseled)
35. rebel + -ing _____ (rebelling)
36. travel + -ing _____ (traveling)
37. develop + -ed _____ (developed)
38. equip + -ment _____ (equipment)
39. develop + -ment _____ (development)
40. cancel + -ation _____ (cancellation)
41. metal + -urgy _____ (metallurgy)
42. tranquil + -ity _____ (tranquillity)
43. tranquil + -ize _____ (tranquilize)
44. chagrin + -ing _____ (chagrining)
45. combat + -ing _____ (combating)
46. bias + -ed _____ (biased)

How to Decide Between *-ence* and *-ance*

PROBLEMS

refer**ence** *or* refer**ance**?
resist**ence** *or* resist**ance**?
abhorr**ance** *or* abhorr**ence**?
persever**ance** *or* persever**ence**?

SOLUTION

Probably the one all-inclusive reason why English spelling seems so illogical and frustrating is that, by the very nature of our language, almost every word in it has come from some foreign tongue.

The great base on which English rests is Anglo-Saxon, which is a combination of *German* dialects.

With the Roman invasion of Britain in early times, followed by Danish and Norman (French) conquerors, our language began to develop along *Latin, Scandinavian*, and *French* lines.

And then, with the revival of learning after the Middle Ages, great numbers of *Latin* and *Greek* terms and roots were used for building the rapidly increasing English vocabulary.

In addition to all of which, English is a thieving kind of language, and has always borrowed flagrantly from *every civilized tongue* and from many primitive ones.

With the result that 95 per cent of our vocabulary has some kind of foreign background.

And, in most cases, though we give a word an Anglicized pronunciation, we faithfully follow the foreign spelling.

It is the foreign spelling that accounts for the middle *s* of *supersede* (Latin *sedeo*, to sit)—

For the *ph* instead of *f* in words like *telephone*, *phonetic*, *symphony*, etc. (all from Greek *phone*, sound).

For the illogical double *t* in *dilettante*[1] (Italian *dilettare*, to delight).

For the illogical double *c* in *desiccate*[2] (Latin *siccus*, dry).

For the -*sy* ending of *ecstasy* (old French *extasie*).

And so on, indefinitely.

It is the foreign derivation which in the main accounts for the endings -ence and -ance.

Which puts Americans without a thorough classical education behind that well-known eight-ball when it comes to deciding whether to end a word with -*ence* or -*ance*.

There is, as it happens, a kind of uniform principle governing the distinction between these endings.

And that is—if the English word ultimately derives from a "first conjugation" Latin verb, the ending is generally -*ance*.

But if the English word ultimately derives from a Latin verb of any other "conjugation," the ending is generally -*ence*.

Which is, I fully and sympathetically admit, no help to you whatever.

For there is no way, unless you are, or have been, a Latin scholar, to determine the "conjugation" of the Latin origin of an English word.

And, in addition, with one minor exception to be noted shortly, there is no other uniform principle (beyond this knowledge of Latin verbs) which will help you make an accurate choice between -*ence* and -*ance*.

---

[1]One who dabbles in the fine arts.
[2]To dry up. Weird as the proper pattern of this obscure word may look, it is correct only with one *s*, two *c*'s.

In this type of problem you will have to rely almost exclusively on developing your visual and kinesthetic responsiveness to a very high degree.

Let us first consider the minor exception.

Which is, that every English verb ending in *r*, preceded by a single vowel, and accented on the last syllable, forms its noun with *-ence.*

We are already quite familiar with this type of verb, having considered it exhaustively in Chapter 22, in which we studied *accent shifts.*

Here, for example, is a fairly complete list.

VERB	NOUN
1. in-fer′	infer**ence** _____
2. pre-fer′	prefer**ence** _____
3. in-cur′	incurr**ence** _____
4. oc-cur′	occurr**ence** _____
5. re-fer′	refer**ence** _____
6. trans-fer′	transfer**ence** _____
7. de-ter′	deterr**ence** _____
8. re-cur′	recurr**ence** _____
9. con-cur′	concurr**ence** _____
10. ab-hor′	abhorr**ence** _____
11. con-fer′	confer**ence** _____
12. de-fer′	defer**ence** _____

On this much, then, you can rely—if the verb is one of the type we have studied in Chapter 22, the noun will definitely end in *-ence* only.

But that's just about as far as we can go with any assurance.

From this point on, you can begin to master the *-ence -ance* problem only by taking two consecutive steps.

Step 1

Determine by the tests that follow which of the commonly confusing *-ence -ance* forms leave you in a dilemma.

Step 2

Concentrate on these personally perplexing nouns, developing, through practice, a keen visual and kinesthetic responsiveness to the correct ending.

Let us see how these steps work out and how effectively they operate for your type of difficulty.

TEST I

Complete these twenty words with either -*ance* or -*ence*, whichever you trust. If in serious doubt, leave the answer blank.

1. admitt- _____	11. repent— _____
2. adher— _____	12. toler— _____
3. compet— _____	13. preval— _____
4. deliver— _____	14. attend— _____
5. confid— _____	15. preced— _____
6. depend— _____	16. extravag— _____
7. persist— _____	17. rever— _____
8. diffid— _____	18. coher— _____
9. opul— _____	19. subsist— _____
10. assur— _____	20. exist— _____

Key to Test 1:

Check your responses against the correct endings below. Where you made an error or left an answer blank, commit the pattern to visual memory and write the correct spelling in the appropriate blank.

1. admitt**ance** _____	11. repent**ance** _____
2. adher**ence** _____	12. toler**ance** _____
3. compet**ence** _____	13. preval**ence** _____
4. deliver**ance** _____	14. attend**ance** _____
5. confid**ence** _____	15. preced**ence** _____
6. depend**ence** _____	16. extravag**ance** _____
7. persist**ence** _____	17. rever**ence** _____

8. diffid**ence** _____   18. coher**ence** _____
9. opul**ence** _____   19. subsist**ence** _____
10. assur**ance** _____   20. exist**ence** _____

The probability is that you made only a few errors, left only a few blanks. For most people, by some strange alchemy, do not have too much trouble with the *-ance -ence* endings, somehow developing, through years of reading and writing, an accurate "feel" for the required ending.

But tighten up your reaction to those errors you did make. Study once again whatever forms caused you trouble, gaining a strong and lasting visual impression.

After you have done that, circle below the numbers of the words on which you erred, and attempt to fill in the correct endings of the circled words. To check your learning, refer again to the key to TEST I, above.

RETEST I

1. admitt _____   11. repent _____
2. adher _____   12. toler _____
3. compet _____   13. preval _____
4. deliver _____   14. attend _____
5. confid _____   15. preced _____
6. depend _____   16. extravag _____
7. persist _____   17. rever _____
8. diffid _____   18. coher _____
9. opul _____   19. subsist _____
10. assur _____   20. exist _____

With some degree of success behind you, you are ready to repeat your training, step by step, on a second group of twenty commonly confusing words.

TEST 2

1. susten _____   3. pertin _____
2. differ _____   4. insist _____

How to Decide Between -ence and -ance

5. contriv _____
6. mainten _____
7. observ _____
8. superintend _____
9. abund _____
10. continu _____
11. resist _____
12. forbear _____

13. appurten _____
14. afflu _____
15. arrog _____
16. protuber _____
17. persever _____
18. relev _____
19. suffer _____
20. petul _____

Key to Test 2

1. sustenance _____
2. difference _____
3. pertinence _____
4. insistence _____
5. contrivance _____
6. maintenance _____
7. observance _____
8. superintendence _____
9. abundance _____
10. continuance _____

11. resistance _____
12. forbearance _____
13. appurtenance _____
14. affluence _____
15. arrogance _____
16. protuberance _____
17. perseverance _____
18. relevance _____
19. sufferance _____
20. petulance _____

RETEST 2

1. susten _____
2. differ _____
3. pertin _____
4. insist _____
5. contriv _____
6. mainten _____
7. observ _____
8. superintend _____
9. abund _____
10. continu _____

11. resist _____
12. forbear _____
13. appurten _____
14. afflu _____
15. arrog _____
16. protuber _____
17. persever _____
18. (ir)relev _____
19. suffer _____
20. petul _____

(Needless to say, if a noun ends in *-ence*, the adjective form similarly ends in *-ent*; and an *-ance* noun likewise has an *-ant* adjective. There is no exception to this principle.)

If you have found that *-ance -ence* confusion is one of your spelling weaknesses, try these final exercises in which the forty troublesome words have been separated into two special groups—those that end in *-ance* and those that end in *-ence*. Take this further opportunity to tighten up your *visual* and *kinesthetic* reactions to each category, at the same time developing an *intellectual* awareness of the grouping to which each word belongs. As in all these exercises, examine the correct pattern for a few seconds, conceal the word, then write it in the blank provided for that purpose.

Group I—*ance* Forms

1. admitt**ance** _____
2. deliver**ance** _____
3. assur**ance** _____
4. repent**ance** _____
5. toler**ance** _____
6. attend**ance** _____
7. extravag**ance** _____
8. susten**ance** _____
9. contriv**ance** _____
10. observ**ance** _____
11. abund**ance** _____
12. continu**ance** _____
13. resist**ance** _____
14. forbear**ance** _____
15. appurten**ance** _____
16. arrog**ance** _____
17. protuber**ance** _____
18. persever**ance** _____
19. (ir)relev**ance** _____
20. suffer**ance** _____
21. petul**ance** _____
22. mainten**ance** _____

Group II—*ence* Forms

1. adher**ence** _____
2. compet**ence** _____
3. confid**ence** _____
4. depend**ence** _____
5. persist**ence** _____
6. diffid**ence** _____
7. opul**ence** _____
8. preval**ence** _____
9. preced**ence** _____
10. rever**ence** _____
11. coher**ence** _____
12. subsist**ence** _____
13. exist**ence** _____
14. differ**ence** _____
15. pertin**ence** _____
16. insist**ence** _____
17. superintend**ence** _____
18. afflu**ence** _____

You have tested yourself on, and begun to master by means of visual, kinesthetic and intellectual attack, forty of the most confusing *-ance -ence* forms.

When you have these forty words under some measure of control—

Plus the twelve *-ence* forms on page 198—

Then you have the fifty-two crucial possibilities of error licked.

Errors are rarely made on any of the other *-ence -ance* forms, but if you should ever find yourself in doubt on some word other than one of the fifty-two covered in this chapter—

Work from the law of mathematical probability.

There are far more words ending in *-ence* than in *ance*.

So, by the law of mathematical probability, you will be reasonably safe in ending the doubtful word with *-ence*.

And let us recall the opening principle of the chapter.

Point 34

Verbs ending in *r*, preceded by a single vowel, and accented on the last syllable, form nouns ending in *-ence* only.

A Footnote to Latin Scholars

(The next paragraph will have meaning for you only if you have studied Latin.)

If you are well acquainted with Latin verbs, you can often rely on the conjugation of the verb to disclose the choice between *-ence* and *-ance*. First conjugation verbs form English nouns ending in *-ance*; second, third, and fourth conjugation verbs form English nouns ending in *-ence*. This rule is not foolproof (*resistere*, for example, produces *resistance*) but works often enough to be useful.

A Footnote to All Readers

With this preliminary visual practice in *-ence -ance* forms, you will notice that your eye will be arrested by almost every *-ence -ance* word you meet in your reading. Do not resist the temptation to linger visually for a few seconds on these words. Such an activity will considerably increase your mastery of all *-ence -ance* nouns, tremendously increase your assurance that you can quickly and successfully make the proper choice when the occasion requires.

PRETEST

1. descend**ent** *or* descend**ant**?
2. inimit**ible** *or* inimit**able**?
3. irrit**ible** *or* irrit**able**?
4. irresist**able** *or* irresist**ible**?
5. vi**l**ify *or* vi**ll**ify?

MNEMONICS

1. (descend**ent** *or* descend**ant**?)

A DESCEND**AN**T is a child, a grandchild, etc. As such he must have an **AN**CESTOR—and the vowel in the first syllable of **AN**CESTOR is of course the key to the puzzling vowel of the last syllable in DESCEND**AN**T.

> *Correct Spelling:* descend**a**nt
> *Mnemonic:* **an**cestor

2. (inimit**ible** *or* inimit**able**?)

Relying on our most useful mnemonic, the linking up of a puzzling spelling to some form of the same word that is easy to spell, the obvious association for the adjective INIMIT**A**BLE is its allied verb form IMIT**A**TE—in both cases the vowel after the *t* is *a*.

> *Correct Spelling:* inimit**a**ble _____
> *Mnemonic:* imit**a**te

3. (irritible *or* irritable)

And for this word we link the adjective form to the verb IRRIT**A**TE, again the vowel *a* after the *t*.

> *Correct Spelling:* irritable _____
> *Mnemonic:* irrit**a**te

4. (irrist**able** *or* irresist**ible**?)

Contradictions abound in English spelling, as you know—

For example:

RESIST**ANCE** ends in *-ance*—

But IRRESIST**IBLE** and its less common affirmative form, RESIST**IBLE**, do not end in *-able*, but in *-ible*.

This is similar to the contradiction you may recall in DEPEND**ABLE**-DEPEND**ENCE**, and is a fairly rare phenomenon, most *-ance* words having the expected *-able* forms, *-ence* words having *-ible* forms.

There are two danger sports in IRR**E**SIST**I**BLE—the fourth and ninth letters, both of which are printed in heavy type. Most common misspelling occurs on the ninth letter, for which an effective mnemonic is L**I**PST**I**CK. Women, let us say, consider that L**I**PST**I**CK helps make them IRR**E**SIST**I**BLE—and as the letter *i* is the only vowel in L**I**PST**I**CK, you will know to use the *-ible* rather than *-able* ending.

There is a somewhat weaker tendency, among inefficient spellers, to pattern IRR**E**SIST**I**BLE very much according to sound, especially in the first two syllables, writing *irrisis-*. To avoid such confusion, realize that you are working from the root R**E**SIST (which no one misspells), plus the negative prefix *ir-*, plus the correct ending *-ible*—result: IR-R**E**SIST-**I**BLE.

(A full exploration of the basic rules that govern all *-able -ible* words will be made in Chapters 28 and 29.)

> *Correct Spellings:* irresist**i**ble _____
> resist**i**ble _____
> *Mnemonic:* l**i**pst**i**ck, r**e**s**i**st

5. (vilify *or* villify?)

This word is accented on the first syllable; it is therefore no wonder that many unsuspecting citizens are seduced into doubling the *l*. However, only one *l* is permitted, owing to its derivation from Latin *vilis, vile*. To VILIFY is to speak evil of, to render VILE—and the related word VILE with one *l*, is the obvious mnemonic.

> *Correct Spelling:* vilify _____
> *Mnemonic:* vile

TEST YOURSELF

I. Check the correct pattern.

1. (a) descendent,	(b) descendant		(b)
2. (a) inimitible,	(b) inimitable		(b)
3. (a) irritible,	(b) irritable		(b)
4. (a) irresistible,	(b) irresistable		(a)
5. (a) vilify,	(b) villify		(a)

II. Recall the mnemonic for each word.

1. vilify _____ (vile)
2. irritable _____ (irritate)
3. irresistible _____ (lipstick, resist)
4. inimitable _____ (imitate)
5. descendant _____ (ancestor)
6. persistent _____ (rent)
7. insistent _____ (rent)
8. superintendent _____ (rent)
9. dependent _____ (rent)
10. dependable _____ (able worker)
11. indispensable _____ (able worker)
12. siege _____ (city)
13. seize _____ (neck)
14. exhilarate _____ (hilarious)
15. battalion _____ (battle)

III. Decide on the missing crucial letter or letters, then rewrite the complete word.

1. descend—nt _____ (a)
2. depend—nt _____ (e)
3. depend—ble _____ (a)
4. indispens—ble _____ (a)
5. s—ge _____ (ie)
6. s—ze _____ (ei)
7. vi—ify _____ (l)
8. ba—a—ion _____ (tt,l)
9. exhi—rate _____ (la)
10. irrit—ble _____ (a)
11. irr—sist—ble _____ (e,i)
12. inimit—ble _____ (a)
13. persist—nt _____ (e)
14. insist—nt _____ (e)
15. superintend—nt _____ (e)

How to Decide Between *-ary* and *-ery*

PROBLEMS

secret**ery** *or* secret**ary**?
monast**ery** *or* monast**ary**?
millin**ery** *or* millin**ary**?

SOLUTION

There are, in all the language, only seven important words that end in *-ery* which might tempt the unsophisticated speller into an *-ary* ending.

(A word like *very*, for extreme example, would not be in this list—no one ever has an urge to spell it *vary*. Nor would anyone be at all likely to write *brewary, bribary, finary, theivary, bakary, flattary,* etc., for the very obviously correct *brewery, bribery, finery, thievery, bakery, flattery,* etc.)

There are, on the other hand, scores and scores of words which correctly end in *-ary* which nevertheless might tempt an unsuspecting citizen into an *-ery* ending.

This fortunate circumstance makes our problem pleasantly simple. You have only to become thoroughly familiar with the seven important *-ery* words—

And then, without further thought, you can spell any other similar *doubt-producing* word with an *-ary* ending.

As it happens, the problem is even simpler than that. Let us look at four of the seven:

distill**ery** _____   millin**ery** _____
station**ery** _____   confection**ery** _____

If you drop the *y* from each of these four, you will be left with common, everyday words describing the performers of an action:

1. distill**er**, one who distills
2. station**er**, one who sells paper, etc.
3. millin**er**, one who makes hats
4. confection**er**, one who makes candies, etc.

In these instances, at least, it is hard to go wrong once you realize that *distillery, stationery, millinery*, and *confectionery* are formed by the simple addition of the letter *y* to the common, shorter forms. The obviously correct *-ery* ending is now too conspicuous to cause any further doubt.

There are three other words, however, with which you will want to develop a strong visual familiarity, words which are not formed by the simple addition of the letter *y* to shorter forms. These three are:

cemet**ery** _____   dysent**ery** _____
monast**ery** _____

And that's all there is to it. Realize that only seven words that end in *-ery* can cause any confusion. Become visually accustomed to the *-ery* ending on each of the seven. And then dismiss the problem from your mind. Every other *doubtful* word probably ends in *-ary*.

Here, for further practice, is another chance for visual and kinesthetic review of the crucial seven:

distill**ery** _____   cemet**ery** _____
station**ery**[1] _____   monast**ery** _____

---

[1] We know from previous work with mnemonics that stationery consists of paper, etc., that stationary means standing still. See Mnemonics—Six.

millin**ery** _____   dysent**ery** _____
confection**ery** _____

There is, then, a very simple basic principle that will effectively solve the problem of this chapter:

Point 35
There are no more than seven *doubtful* words which require -*ery* as terminal letters—in any others, if doubt exists, use -*ary*.

TEST YOURSELF

Decide, in the following words, whether -*ery* or -*ary* is the required ending, then rewrite the complete word.

  1. diction— _____   (diction**ary**)
  2. station— _____   (station**ery**)
      (paper, etc.)
  3. secret— _____   (secret**ary**)
  4. confection— _____   (confection**ery**)
  5. dignit— _____   (dignit**ary**)
  6. cemet— _____   (cemet**ery**)
  7. sedent— _____   (sedent**ary**)
  8. distill— _____   (distill**ery**)
  9. statu— _____   (statu**ary**)
10. monast— _____   (monast**ery**)
11. discretion— _____   (discrtion**ary**)
12. dysent— _____   (dysent**ery**)
13. comment— _____   (comment**ary**)
14. millin— _____   (millin**ery**)
15. advers— _____   (advers**ary**)
16. station— _____   (station**ary**)
      (motionless)

MNEMONICS
Ten *(Eighteenth Day, continued)*

PRETEST

1. whisky *or* whiskey?
2. tyranny *or* tyrrany?
3. difinately *or* definitely?
4. proffesor *or* professor?
5. drunkeness, drunkedness, *or* drunkness?

MNEMONICS

1. (whisky *or* whiskey?)

Which is correct—*whisky* or *whiskey*?

In a sense, both are correct—and you may, if you wish to insist on your rights, use whichever form appeals to you.

However, by a common custom in the liquor trade, the shorter spelling is used for one type, the longer spelling for another type.

Obviously, the type of liquor that would be most frugal in the number of letters in its name is Scotch—for which the traditional spelling is WHIS**KY**—plural: WHIS-**KIES**. (Canadian liquor is also spelled WHIS**KY**.) On the other hand, any American brand is WHIS**KEY**—plural; WHIS**KEYS**.

You may check this distinction next time you have access to a bottle of Scotch, rye, bourbon, etc.

But I suggest you make the check *before* you sample the contents—afterward you won't really care.

Correct Spellings: Scotch or
Canadian whisky _____
domestic whiskey _____
Mnemonic: Scotch is the more frugal spelling.

2. (tyranny *or* tyrrany?)

TYRANT is practically never misspelled—one is rarely tempted to use more than one *r* in this common word.

Yet the related forms TYRANNY, TYRANNOUS, and TYRANNICAL cause confusion among the most sophisticated of spellers.

The simple and effective mnemonic for all three difficult forms is the phrase "DOWN WITH TYRANTS!" This phrase, when viewed as a unit, contains two *n*'s (one in DOWN, one more in TYRANTS), and one *r*—the correct combination in each of these three confusing words.

Correct Spellings: tyranny _____
tyrannous _____
tyrannical _____
Mnemonic: "Down with tyrants!"

3. (definately *or* definitely?)

In this word, the crucial letter is the vowel after the *n*. Link DEFINITELY with the associated form DEFINITION or FINITE.

Correct Spelling: definitely _____
Mnemonics: definition, finite

4. (proffesor *or* professor?)

What, in a sense, does a PROFESSOR do? His job, you might say, is to PROFESS—and the pronunciation of the verb PROFESS is such that no combination other than one *f* and two *s*'s makes sense. Link PROFESSOR to PROFESS and you can avoid confusion as to which consonant requires doubling.

Correct Spelling: pro**fess**or _____
Mnemonic: pro**fess**

5. (drunke**n**ess, drunke**dn**ess, *or* drun**kn**ess?)

This word is one of the ten most frequently misspelled—and no wonder. The first part is simple enough—DRUNK, obviously. Just as obviously, the ending is -NESS. But what, if anything, happens in between?

Well, from educated adults to whom I propound this question I receive, generally, one of the following answers.

> *drunkness*   *drunkeness*
> *drunkardness*   *drunkedness*

None of these, unfortunately, is the correct pattern—and all of them are popular, *drunkeness* being the most prevalent misspelling.

The word is properly spelled by analogy with *suddenness* (*sudden* plus -*ness*) *barrenness* (*barren* plus -*ness*), *commonness* (*common* plus -*ness*), etc. The only correct pattern, then, is DRUNK<u>ENN</u>ESS (*drunken* plus -*ness*) —all the others, logical and sound though they may seem, are totally incorrect and unacceptable.

Correct Spelling: drunk**enn**ess _____
Mnemonic: drunk**en** plus -**n**ess

(All the patterns offered in the pretest were incorrect.)

TEST YOURSELF

I. Check the correct pattern.
1. Scotch (a) whisky, (b) whiskey   (a)
2. (a) tyranny, (b) tyrrany   (a)
3. (a) professor, (b) proffesor   (a)
4. (a) definately, (b) definitely   (b)
5. (a) drunkenness, (b) drunkeness   (a)

II. Recall the mnemonic for each word. (Complete Review.)
1. occu**rr**ence _____ (cu**rr**ent event)
2. superintend**ent** _____ (**rent**)

3. inoculate _____ (inject)
4. indispensable _____ (able worker)
5. dependable) _____ (able worker)
6. siege _____ (city)
7. seize _____ (neck)
8. battalion _____ (battle)
9. parallel _____ (all tracks)
10. fricassee _____ (casserole)
11. persistent _____ (rent)
12. insistent _____ (rent)
13. dependent _____ (rent)
14. embarrassed _____ (two robbers, Sing Sing, ass)
15. anoint _____ (an oil)
16. exhilarate _____ (hilarious)
17. vicious _____ (vice)
18. ridiculous _____ (ridicule)
19. description _____ (describe)
20. repetition _____ (repeat)
21. recommend _____ (commend)
22. business _____ (busy)
23. absence _____ (absent)
24. holiday _____ (holy)
25. despair _____ (desperate)
26. all right _____ (all wrong)
27. balloon _____ (ball)
28. pursuit _____ (purse)
29. sheriff _____ (riff raff)
30. category _____ (section)
31. occasional _____ (measure)
32. vacuum _____ (vacant)
33. stationary _____ (stand)
34. stationery _____ (paper)
35. principal _____ (main)
36. principle _____ (rule)
37. separate _____ (apart)

38. accelerate _____ (celerity)
39. devise _____ (devious)
40. iridescent _____ (iris)
41. tranquillity _____ (**quill**)
42. grammar _____ (**mar**)
43. pronunciation _____ (pro-**NUN**-ci-a-tion)
44. sacrilegious _____ (sac-ri-**LE**-gious)
45. genealogy _____ (ge-ne-**AL**-o-gy)
46. mineralogy _____ (min-er-**AL**-o-gy)
47. maintenance _____ (main-**ten**-ance)
48. descendant _____ (**an**cestor)
49. inimitable _____ (imitate)
50. irritable _____ (irritate)
51. irresistible _____ (lipstick)
52. vilify _____ (vile)
53. whisky _____ (Scotch)
54. whiskey _____ (domestic)
55. tyranny, _____ ("Down with
 etc. Tyrants!")
56. professor _____ (to profess)
57. drunkenness _____ (drunken + -ness)
58. definitely _____ (definition;
 finite)

III. Decide on the crucial missing letter or letters, then rewrite the complete word. (Complete Review.)

1. occu—nce _____ (rre)
2. superintend—nt _____ (e)
3. i—o—ulate _____ (n,c)
4. indispens—ble _____ (a)
5. depend—ble _____ (a)
6. s—ge _____ (ie)
7. s—ze _____ (ei)
8. ba—a—ion _____ (tt,l)
9. para—e— _____ (ll,l)
10. fri—a—ee— _____ (c,ss)

11. persist—nt _____ (e)
12. insist—nt _____ (e)
13. depend—nt _____ (e)
14. emba—a—ed _____ (rr,ss)
15. a—oint _____ (n)
16. exhi—rate _____ (la)
17. vi—ious _____ (c)
18. r—diculous _____ (i)
19. d—scription _____ (e)
20. rep—tition _____ (e)
21. re—o—end _____ (c,mm)
22. bu—ness _____ (si)
23. abs—nce _____ (e)
24. ho—iday _____ (l)
25. d—spair _____ (e)
26. a—right _____ (ll)
27. ba—oon _____ (ll)
28. p—rsuit _____ (u)
29. sher— _____ (iff)
30. cat—gory _____ (e)
31. occa—ional _____ (s)
32. va—uum _____ (c)
33. station—ry _____ (a)
    (fixed)
34. station—ry _____ (e)
    (paper)
35. princip— _____ (al)
    (main)
36. princip— _____ (le)
    (rule)
37. sep—rate _____ (a)
38. acce—erate _____ (l)
39. d—vise _____ (e)
40. i—idescent _____ (r)
41. tranqui—ity _____ (ll)
42. gramm—r _____ (a)

43. pron—nciation _____ (u)
44. sacr—l—gious _____ (i,e)
45. gene—logy _____ (a)
46. miner—logy _____ (a)
47. maint—nance _____ (e)
48. descend—nt _____ (a)
49. inimit—ble _____ (a)
50. irrit—ble _____ (a)
51. irresist—ble _____ (i)
52. vi—ify _____ (l)
53. whisk—(Scotch) _____ (y)
54. whisk—(others) _____ (ey)
55. ty—a—y _____ (r,nn)
56. pro—e—or _____ (f,ss)
57. drunk—ess _____ (enn)
58. defin—ly _____ (ite)

How to Make an Accurate Decision Between -*able* and -*ible*

PROBLEM

detest**able** *or* detest**ible**?
irrit**able** *or* irrit**ible**?
abomin**able** *or* abomin**ible**?
predict**able** *or* predict**ible**?

SOLUTION

A word may correctly end in -*able*, say *detestable* or *presentable*.

Another word may correctly end in -*ible*, say *digestible* or *corruptible*.

The last syllables of all four words are identical in pronunciation—yet for two of them we write -*able*, for the other two -*ible*.

Why?

The final answer often lies in the Latin derivation of the word, as it does in -*ence* -*ance* forms—but it would then seem that only a scholar of the classics would be able unerringly to make an accurate and self-assured choice.

Which would be unfortunate—for there are so many hundreds of words that end in either -*able* or -*ible*, most of them common enough to be used over and over again in everyday writing, that only the Latin students could be expected to write an error-free paper.

Fortunately there is a fact which weighs heavily in favor of your learning to feel completely in control of the *-able -ible* problem even if you have never studied Latin.

This fact is:

With no more than a normal number of exceptions, all -able and -ible words fall into easily learned and sharply differentiated groups.

To the uninitiated, the problem of whether to end a word with *-able* or *-ible* is a source of never-ending confusion—

To the sophisticated speller who is familiar with basic principles of English spelling patterns, it is no problem at all.

And it need be no problem to you—

If you become thoroughly familiar with every relevant characteristic of each of the *-able* and *-ible* groups—

And if, in addition—

You make a complete intellectual, visual, and kinesthetic adjustment to the typical examples that will be offered·in each group.

As a result of such training, you will eventually be able to put all doubts and hesitation out of your mind when you have to decide between ending a word with *-able* or *-ible*.

A big promise? Yes, but in this instance easy to fulfill.

If we thread our way cautiously and patiently through the applicable principles, as we usually do, a seemingly complicated and troublesome problem can be mastered with almost no pain.

Follow me carefully, now, step by step.

We shall consider in this chapter six groups of *-able* words.

Group I. The Root Is a Full Word
    Notice these typical examples:

detest**able** _____   perish**able** _____
predict**able** _____   person**able** _____

avail**able** _____ correct**able** _____

depend**able** _____ detect**able** _____

You will observe, in each case, that if you drop the -*able* ending you have left a full, acceptable, everyday word:

detest	avail	perish	correct
predict	depend	person	detect

Which permits us to formulate a basic principle:

Point 36

Roots usually end in -*able* if, in their own right, they are full, acceptable English words.

Here are some more examples out of hundreds. Drop the -*able* in each case and a full word is left.

mail**able** _____ present**able** _____

profit**able** _____ credit**able** _____

accept**able** _____ break**able** _____

etc.

Group II. The Root is a Full Word Lacking Final e

Now examine these typical examples:

blam**able** _____ debat**able** _____

deplor**able** _____ excit**able** _____

desir**able** _____ presum**able** _____

You will observe here a new common factor—if you drop -*able* you have left a root lacking only a final -*e* to be a full word:

blam(e)	*desir(e)*	*excit(e)*
deplor(e)	*debat(e)*	*presum(e)*

Which permits us to formulate our second principle:

Point 37

Forms usually are spelled with an -*able* ending if the root needs only a final -*e* to be a full word.

Here are more and similar examples to illustrate Point 37: Note, in each case, that if -*able* is dropped a full word lacking only final -*e* remains.

lov**able** _____   valu**able** _____

pleasur**able** _____   us**able** _____

siz**able** _____   (in)describ**able** _____

Group III. The Root Ends in i

Examine these words, looking again for a comon element:

appreci**able** _____   reli**able** _____

envi**able** _____   satisfi**able** _____

justifi**able** _____   soci**able** _____

Impossible to escape is the common letter *i* preceding each ending. Obviously -*able* is the only sane suffix, else we would have a double *i*, a scarce and un-American combination. So we now have a third basic principle:

Point 38
-*able* is always found after the letter *i*.

Group IV. The Root Has Other Forms Built on the Letter -*a*

Consider these typical examples:

demonstr**able** _____   irrit**able** _____

dur**able** _____   inviol**able** _____

repar**able** _____   inflamm**able** _____

Here the common element may be somewhat less easy to detect. When we drop -*able*, we do not have a full word left, with or without an added *e*—but suppose we think of other forms of these words:

(demonstr**able**) demonstrate   (irrit**able**) irritate
(dur**able**) duration   (inviol**able**) violate
(repar**able**) reparations   (inflamm**able**) inflammation

And there it is, the common element we've been looking for—each root can be formed into a word containing as a principal vowel the letter *a*—hence the ending *-able*. So we can now understand a fourth basic principle:

Point 39

A root will generally require an *-able* ending if there are other forms of the word which contain *a* as the principal vowel.

Take some more examples to illustrate Point 39.

(pregnant) impregn**able** _____
(delectation) delect**able** _____
(hospitality) hospit**able** _____
(penetrate) impenetr**able** _____
(abomination) abomin**able** _____
(estimate) estim**able** _____
(imitate) inimit**able**) _____
(tolerate) intoler**able** _____
(separate) insepar**able** _____
(enumerate) innumer**able** _____

Group V. The Root Ends in Hard c *or* g

Notice, in the following forms, the letter preceding *-able*, and pay particular attention to how that letter is pronounced:

despic**able** _____ applic**able** _____
educ**able** _____ amic**able** _____
implac**able** _____ practic**able** _____
explic**able** _____ navig**able** _____
revoc**able** _____ indefatig**able** _____

The letter preceding the *-able* ending is in each instance either *c* or *g*; moreover, both letters have hard pronunciations—*c* as in *cat*, *g* as in *go*.

Now this is no surprise.

We know from earlier chapters that *a* is a hardening

vowel—if *c* or *g* is hard in pronunciation, only *-able* will retain this hardness; *-ible* (since the letter *i* is a softening vowel) will soften a letter which we wish to keep hard.

So we can easily formulate a fifth principle:

Point 40:
-able is the only possible ending after a hard *c* or *g*, in order to maintain the required pronunciation.

These five groupings have taken care of whatever uniformities exist in *-able* patterns—

They give you a good, fast, running start on making an accurate decision as to whether to end a word with *-able* or *-ible*.

For you know that *-able* is probably[1] the required ending under *any one* of the following circumstances:

1. If the root is a full word in its own right (*govern*-able, *impression*-able, *respect*-able, etc.)

2. If the root is a full word lacking only the final *e* (*blam*-able, *believ*-able, *palat*-able, etc.)

3. If the preceding letter is *i*, in order to avoid a double *i* combination (*soci*-able, *justifi*-able, *certifi*-able, etc.)

4. If the root has another form built on *a* as the principal vowel (irritable—irritate, demonstrable—demonstrate, etc.)

5. If the preceding letter is a *c* or *g* that is pronounced hard (applicable, navigable, etc.)

These five points alone can give you self-assured command over several hundred *-able* words—only a few of the available examples were used to illustrate each principle.

Group VI. Exceptional Cases
There are a number of important words ending in *-able* which do not fit into any of the five groups discussed.

---

[1] I say "probably" because of course there will be exceptions to some of these principles. These we shall consider in due time.

How to Make an Accurate Decision Between -able and -ible

These you have no choice but to become familiar with *visually*, so that only *-able* looks proper and *-ible* seems unfamiliar, unpleasant, and therefore incorrect.

I'll list the words—commit each one as firmly as you can to visual memory, writing each form in the blank provided.

1. equit**able** _____
2. formid**able** _____
3. inexor**able** _____
4. inevit**able** _____
5. memor**able** _____
6. prob**able** _____
7. unconscion**able** _____
8. port**able** _____
9. ar**able** _____
10. ineff**able** _____
11. pot**able** _____
12. inscrut**able** _____
13. insuper**able** _____
14. indomit**able** _____
15. malle**able** _____
16. vulner**able** _____
17. aff**able** _____
18. palp**able** _____
19. culp**able** _____

(These nineteen words fit into no particular category—they must be learned individually.)

How to Recognize a Root That Requires an *-ible* Suffix

PROBLEMS

collaps**able** *or* collaps**ible**?
contempt**able** *or* contempt**ible**?
resist**able** *or* resist**ible**?
connect**able** *or* connect**ible**?

SOLUTION

You know that if a root is a full word, or a full word except for the final *e*, the likely ending will be *-able*.

You know, also, that *-able* attaches to three types of roots that are not full words:

1. Those that end in the letter *i*—

(*insati-***able**, etc.)

2. Those that have other forms built on *a* as the principal vowel—

(inimit**able**—imit**a**te, etc.)

3. Those that end in *hard c* or *g*—

(irrevo**cable**, indefati**gable**, etc.)

226

And you know, also, that there are nineteen special *-able* roots which are not full words and do not fit into any of the three categories listed above.

All right—that should be clear enough by now.

And there should be an equally clear implication that *-ible* is the proper ending for roots which are *not* full words (or full words lacking final *e*), and which do not end in the letter *i* or in hard *c* or *g*, and which furthermore do not belong among the nineteen special cases considered in the previous chapter.

Note, then, how the following *-ible* forms are built on "non-word" roots which do not fit into any previously established *-able* categories. (The root is italicized so that you can see at a glance that it is not, by itself, a real word.)

Group I. The Root Is Not a Full Word

aud **ible** _____	*ostens* **ible** _____
compat **ible** _____	*poss* **ible** _____
cred **ible** _____	*terr* **ible** _____
divis **ible** _____	*horr* **ible** _____
vis **ible** _____	*dirig* **ible** _____
feas **ible** _____	*neglig* **ible** _____
plaus **ible** _____	*ed* **ible** _____
combust **ible** _____	*infall* **ible** _____
suscept **ible** _____	*tang* **ible** _____
ris **ible** _____	*intellig* **ible** _____
incorrig **ible** _____	*indel* **ible** _____
irasc **ible** _____	

These are by no means all, or even most, of the *-ible* forms which are built on non-word roots; but there are enough to emphasize that non-word roots *other than the -able types we have discussed* can be presumed to require an *-ible* ending. We can, in fact, now formulate our first basic *-ible* principle:

Point 41

Non-word roots which do not fall into previous *-able* categories will require an *-ible* ending.

You realize now that special kinds of non-word roots take *-able*, that otherwise a non-word root takes *-ible*.

The next question that may occur to you is, do all *full-word* roots require *-able*?

The answer, unfortunately, is no.

There is a special type of full-word root which ends in *-ible*.

Namely, that root which forms a noun by the *immediate* addition of the suffix *-ion*.

For example:

    (collect—collec*tion*) collect**ible** _____
    (digest—diges*tion*) digest**ible** _____
    (corrupt-corrup*tion*) corrupt**ible** _____
    (exhaust—exhaus*tion*) inexhaust**ible** _____

Notice that I say "by the *immediate* addition of the suffix *-ion*."

So that roots like *expect, excite, detest, present*, etc., would not fit into this category. Notice that such roots add *-ation*, not an immediate *-ion*:

    (expect—expect*ation*) expect**able** _____
    (detest—detest*ation*) detest**able** _____
    (present—present*ation*) present**able** _____
    (excite—excit*ation*) excit**able** _____

Now examine the type of root which adds an immediate *-ion* suffix:

Group II. The Root Is a Full Word That Has an Immediate -ion Form

    (collect—collec*tion*) collect**ible** _____
    (digest—diges*tion*) digest**ible** _____
    (corrupt—corrup*tion*) corrupt**ible** _____

How to Recognize a Root That Requires an *-ible* Suffix

(exhaust—exhaust*ion*) (in)exhaust**ible** _____

(affect—affec*tion*) affect**ible** _____

(contract—contrac*tion*) contract**ible** _____

(connect—connec*tion*) connect**ible** _____

(convert—conver*sion*[1]) convert**ible** _____

(access—acces*sion*) access**ible** _____

(corrode—corro*sion*[2]) corrod**ible** _____

(expanse—expan*sion*) expans**ible** _____

(perfect—perfec*tion*) perfect**ible** _____

(reverse—rever*sion*) revers**ible** _____

(suggest—sugges*tion*) suggest**ible** _____

But how about *predict, detect,* and *correct*?

These words have immediate *-ion* forms: *prediction, detection, correction.*

And yet they have *-able* endings!

Namely:

predict**able** _____   correct**able** _____

detect**able** _____

So these three have to be considered special exceptions, and we would formulate our basic principles as follows:

Point 42

With the exception of *predictable, detectable,* and *correctable*, a full-word root that can add an immediate *-ion* is likely to have an *-ible* ending.

You know so far the *non-word roots*, other than special types, take an *-ible* ending.

And you know that *full-word roots* that have immediate *-ion* forms also take an *-ible* ending (excepting *predictable, correctable,* and *detectable*).

Let us now examine a third type of *-ible* word.

---

[1] *t* changes to *s*, which does not alter the principle.

[2] *d* changes to *s*, which again does not affect the principle.

Group III. The Root Ends in -ns *or* -miss

defe*ns*i**ble** _____	reprehe*ns*i**ble** _____
indefe*ns*i**ble** _____	se*ns*i**ble** _____
comprehe*ns*i**ble** _____	inse*ns*i**ble** _____
incomprehe*ns*i**ble** _____	expa*ns*i**ble** _____
respo*ns*i**ble** _____	trans*miss*i**ble** _____
irrespo*ns*i**ble** _____	ad*miss*i**ble** _____
oste*ns*i**ble** _____	per*miss*i**ble** _____
diste*ns*i**ble** _____	dis*miss*i**ble** _____

This is simple enough. While some of these words would also fit into Groups I or II (the root of *comprehensible* is not a full word; the root of *admissible* has an immediate *-ion* ending—*admission*, etc.), still an *-ns* or *-miss* root immediately alerts you to end your word in *-ible* rather than *-able*.

Except, of course, for our old friend INDISPENS**ABLE**!

You see, now, why the temptation is so great to use an *-ible* ending on this word—practically every other *-ns* form requires it.

But *indispensable* links up with *dependable* and is a word over which the mnemonic "**ABLE** worker" has given you full control.

So we are ready for our third basic principle:

Point 43

If the root ends in *-ns* or *-miss*, use *-ible*, except in *indispensable* (or, of course, *dispensable*).

Our next type of *-ible* words may also fit into previous categories, but will contain so conspicuous a common factor that we shall examine it in a separate group.

Group IV. The Root Ends in Soft c *or* g

invin**cible** _____	convin**cible** _____
for**cible** _____	redu**cible** _____
coer**cible** _____	irredu**cible** _____

sedu**cible** _____   produ**cible** _____
indu**cible** _____   incorri**gible** _____
dedu**cible** _____   intan**gible** _____
negli**gible** _____   intelli**gible** _____
eli**gible** _____   le**gible** _____

ille**gible** _____

In each of these instances the *c* is pronounced soft—like an *s*; or the *g* is pronounced soft—like a *j*. If *-able* were the suffix, *c* and *g* would be hard—clearly only *-ible* is possible.

These words will of course remind you of those demons with soft *c* and *g* which we discussed in Chapters 12 and 14. There the correct ending was *-able* and the *e* had to be retained to keep *c* or *g* soft. You will recall:

enfor**ceable** _____   char**geable** _____
embra**ceable** _____   brid**geable** _____
la**ceable** _____   chan**geable** _____
repla**ceable** _____   mana**geable** _____
irrepla**ceable** _____   dispara**geable** _____
pronoun**ceable** _____   enga**geable** _____
tra**ceable** _____   discoura**geable** _____
servi**ceable** _____   marria**geable** _____
boun**ceable** _____   enra**geable** _____
pea**ceable** _____   salva**geable** _____
noti**ceable** _____   mortga**geable** _____

jud**geable** _____

This need not be at all confusing. You have already made a strong adjustment to the *-ceable* and *-geable* words of Chapters 12 and 14, and these new *-cible* and *-gible* words can be easily separated in your mind from the previous groups you have studied.

To begin with, notice that every *-ceable* and *-geable* root is a word in its own right if final *-e* is retained: *enforce, embrace, notice, charge, change, marriage,* etc.

But of the *-cible* and *-gible* roots only the *duc-* forms plus three others (*coerce—coercible, force—forcible, convince—convincible*) are full words if final *-e* is retained.

Keeping these factors in mind, let us formulate our next basic principle:

Point 44

Roots ending in soft *-c* or soft *-g* require the *-ible* ending. These roots are usually not full words, with the exception of *coercible, forcible, convincible,* and the *-ducible* group.

Group V. Exceptional Cases

We are ready, now, for the comparatively few instances of *-ible* words which do not fit into one of the four previous groups. Like the nineteen special *-able* words, these too must be mastered by visual and kinesthetic memory.

1. contempt**ible** _____
2. gull**ible** _____
3. collaps**ible** _____
4. flex**ible** _____

4. inflex**ible** _____
6. resist**ible** _____
7. irresist**ible** _____
8. discern**ible** _____

Eight forms, all of them full words when the ending is dropped (*contempt-**ible**, gull-**ible**, discern-**ible**, resist-**ible**,* etc.). And no root has an *-ion* form. So they should all be *-able* forms—that they are not makes them exceptional cases.

Let us now chart, for quick and successful review, all we know about *-able* and *-ible* words.

COMPLETE LAYOUT ON *-able* AND *-ible* WORDS

THE *-ABLE* ENDING IS ATTACHED TO:	THE *-IBLE* ENDING IS ATTACHED TO:
1. Roots that are full words in their own right —*surmount*-able, etc.	1. Roots that are not full words in their own right —*vis*-ible, etc. *EXCEPT* special "non-word" *-able* forms.

How to Recognize a Root That Requires an *-ible* Suffix

COMPLETE LAYOUT ON *-able* AND *-ible* WORDS
(*continued*)

THE -ABLE ENDING IS ATTACHED TO:	THE *-IBLE* ENDING IS ATTACHED TO:
2. Roots that are full words lacking only final *e*. —*ador(e)*-able, etc.	2. Roots that are full words in their own right and which have immediate *-ion* forms —*express-ion*-inexpressible, etc. *EXCEPT predictable, detectable,* and *correctable.*
3. Roots ending in the letter *-i*. —*ami*-able, etc.	3. Roots that end in *-ns* or *-miss*—defens-ible, admiss-ible, etc. *EXCEPT dispensable* and *indispensable.*
4. Roots that have other forms built on *-a* as the principal vowel. —*cap*able—cap*a*city, etc.	4. No similar category.
5. Roots that end in *hard* *-c* or *-g*—commu*i*nicable, navigable, etc.	5. Roots that end in *soft -c* or *-g*—seducible, negligible, etc. These roots are usually not full words, with the exception of *coercible*[1], *forcible*[1], *convincible*[1], and the *-ducible* group.
6. Roots that keep the softening *-e* after *-c* or *-g*—noti*ce*able, mana*ge*able, etc.	6. No similar category.

[1]When final *-e* is replaced, we have *coerce, force, convince,* etc.

233

And recall the nineteen exceptional cases under *-able*, the eight exceptional cases under *-ible*. Let us review these once again:

-ABLE FORMS

1. equit**able** _____
2. formid**able** _____
3. inexor**able** _____
4. inevit**able** _____
5. memor**able** _____
6. prob**able** _____
7. unconscion**able** _____
8. port**able** _____
9. ar**able** _____
10. ineff**able** _____
11. pot**able** _____
12. inscrut**able** _____
13. insuper**able** _____
14. indomit**able** _____
15. malle**able** _____
16. vulner**able** _____
17. aff**able** _____
18. palp**able** _____

19. culp**able** _____

-IBLE FORMS

1. contempt**ible** _____
2. gull**ible** _____
3. flex**ible** _____
4. inflex**ible** _____
5. collaps**ible** _____
6. discern**ible** _____
7. resist**ible** _____
8. irresist**ible** _____

TEST YOURSELF

Add the correct ending (*-able* or *-ible*) to the following roots, rewriting the complete word.

I. Full Words

1. depend— _____ (able)
2. companion— _____ (able)
3. detest— _____ (able)
4. predict— _____ (able)
5. detect— _____ (able)
6. correct— _____ (able)
7. present— _____ (able)
8. remark— _____ (able)

How to Recognize a Root That Requires an *-ible* Suffix

    9. miser— _____ (able)
  10. pass— _____ (able)

II. Root a Full Word Lacking -e
  11. excit— _____ (able)
  12. lov— _____ (able)
  13. argu— _____ (able)
  14. excus— _____ (able)
  15. mov— _____ (able)
  16. desir— _____ (able)
  17. valu— _____ (able)
  18. ador— _____ (able)
  19. deplor— _____ (able)
  20. debat— _____ (able)

III. Root Ends in -i
  21. ami— _____ (able)
  22. soci— _____ (able)
  23. classifi— _____ (able)
  24. envi— _____ (able)

IV. Root Has Other Forms Built on the Letter -a
  25. commend—(commend*a*tion) _____ (able)
  26. irrit—(irrit*a*tion) _____ (able)
  27. cap—(cap*a*city) _____ (able)
  28. (in)separ—(separ*a*te) _____ (able)
  29. (in)toler—(toler*a*te) _____ (able)

V. Root Ends in Hard -c or -g
  30. applic— _____ (able)
  31. explic— _____ (able)
  32. navig— _____ (able)
  33. indefatig— _____ (able)
  34. revoc— _____ (able)
  35. implac— _____ (able)

VI. Root is a "Non-Word"
  36. aud— _____ (ible)
  37. plaus— _____ (ible)

38. feas— _____ (ible)
39. ris— _____ (ible)
40. horr— _____ (ible)
41. combust— _____ (ible)

VII. Root Has an -ion Form
42. collect—(collection) _____ (ible)
43. indestruct—(destruction) _____ (ible)
44. convert—(conversion) _____ (ible)
45. incorrupt—(corruption) _____ (ible)

VIII. Root Ends in Soft -c or -g
46. evinc— _____ (ible)
47. forc— _____ (ible)
48. neglig— _____ (ible)
49. intellig— _____ (ible)
50. elig— _____ (ible)
51. irreduc— _____ (ible)
52. illeg— _____ (ible)
53. intang— _____ (ible)
54. incorrig— _____ (ible)

IX. Root Ends in Soft -c or -g and Retains the -e
55. enforce— _____ (able)
56. notice— _____ (able)
57. manage— _____ (able)
58. change— _____ (able)
59. marriage— _____ (able)

X. Exceptional Cases
60. port— _____ (able)
61. inevit— _____ (able)
62. formid— _____ (able)
63. insuper— _____ (able)
64. vulner— _____ (able)
65. aff— _____ (able)
66. culp— _____ (able)
67. contempt— _____ (ible)

How to Recognize a Root That Requires an *-ible* Suffix

68. flex— _____ (ible)
69. collaps— _____ (ible)
70. (ir)resist— _____ (ible)
71. discern— _____ (ible)

XI. Root Ends in -ns or -miss

72. (in)defense— _____ (ible)
73. reprehens— _____ (ible)
74. (ir)respons— _____ (ible)
75. (in)sens— _____ (ible)
76. (in)comprehens— _____ (ible)
77. admiss— _____ (ible)
78. permiss— _____ (ible)
79. transmiss— _____ (ible)
80. (in)dispens— _____ (able)
81. ostens— _____ (ible)

30 *(Nineteenth Day, concluded)*

How to Decide Between *-er* and *-or*

PROBLEM

commentate**r** *or* commentat**or**?
elevate**r** *or* elevat**or**?
visite**r** *or* visit**or**?
bette**r** *or* bett**or**?

SOLUTION

The *-or -er* problem is not so common that we need make a big thing out of it. Both suffixes mean either "one who" or "that which" (*investor*, one who *invests*; *elevator*, that which *raises*), and there is no uniformity governing the use of the proper ending. *-Er* is the sensible form, since it follows the pronunciation—but far more words end in *-or* than in *-er*. Most educated people have developed an unconscious visual reaction to *-er -or* words, and have trouble only with a few isolated forms.

And their trouble always takes this shape: they are tempted to write *-er* when *-or* is correct, rarely the other way around.

So a good, serviceable, trustworthy principle can be formulated:

Point 45

When in doubt, use *-or* rather than *-er* as an ending with the meaning of "one who" or "that which."

Let me present twenty of the occasionally troublesome forms. Develop a keen visual reaction to them, practice each one kinesthetically, and the chances are very good that this problem, if it is present at all, will vanish.

Occasionally Misspelled Words Ending in -or

1. aviat**or** _____
2. educat**or** _____
3. distribut**or** _____
4. elevat**or** _____
5. escalat**or** _____
6. impost**or** _____
7. indicat**or** _____
8. investigat**or** _____
9. commentat**or** _____
10. predecess**or** _____
11. radiat**or** _____
12. supervis**or** _____
13. surviv**or** _____
14. visit**or** _____
15. prevaricat**or** _____
16. fabricat**or** _____
17. accelerat**or** _____
18. protect**or** _____
19. spectat**or** _____
20. administrat**or** _____

And of course there is also *bettor*, one who makes a *bet*, not to be confused with *better*, the comparative of *good*.

TEST YOURSELF

Add the proper ending (*-or* or *-er*) to each root; then rewrite the complete word.

1. surviv— _____ (or)
2. administrat— _____ (or)
3. spectat— _____ (or)
4. protect— _____ (or)
5. accelerat— _____ (or)
6. fabricat— _____ (or)
7. prevaricat— _____ (or)

8. visit— _____ (or)
9. supervis— _____ (or)
10. radiat— _____ (or)
11. predecess— _____ (or)
12. commentat— _____ (or)
13. investigat— _____ (or)
14. indicat— _____ (or)
15. impost— _____ (or)
16. escalat— _____ (or)
17. elevat— _____ (or)
18. distribut— _____ (or)
19. educat— _____ (or)
20. aviat— _____ (or)

Fourth Review

And now your training is complete.

In chapters 26–30 we have covered the basic principles that govern the remaining problems— *-ance* or *-ence?*, *-ary* or *-ery?*, *-able* or *-ible?*, and *-er* or *-or?*

As to the problem of *-ance* or *-ence*, you have learned:
1. That the special group of verbs which end in single *-r* preceded by a single vowel, *and accented on the final syllable*, all form nouns in *-ence*.

 refer**ence** _____   abhorr**ence** _____
                          etc.

2. That otherwise only visual and kinesthetic practice can help you make a correct choice.
3. And that, if you are still in serious doubt, *-ence* is the likely ending, owing to its greater numerical occurrence.

As to the problem of *-ary* or *-ery*, you have learned:
4. That *-ary* is by far the commoner ending.
5. But that *-ery* is correct in seven important words, namely:

1. distill**ery** _____   4. confection**ery** _____
2. station**ery** _____   5. cemet**ery** _____
   (paper)   6. monast**ery** _____
3. millin**ery** _____   7. dysent**ery** _____

As to the problem of -*able* or -*ible*, you have learned:

6. That -*able* attaches to most full-word roots.

predict-**able** _____ depend-**able** _____
etc.

7. That -*able* attaches to most full-word roots lacking only final -*e*.

deplor(e)-**able** _____ debat(e)-**able** _____
etc.

8. That -*able* attaches to roots ending in the letter -*i*.

justifi-**able** _____ reli-**able** _____
etc.

9. That -*able* attaches to roots which have other forms built on -*a* as a principal vowel.

(imitate) inimit**able** ___ (irritate) irrit**able** _____
etc.

10. That -*able* attaches to roots ending in hard -*c* or -*g*.

navig**able** _____ practic**able** _____

11. And that, finally, -*able* attaches to nineteen special roots which have no common characteristics. These are:

1. equit**able** _____	11. pot**able** _____
2. formid**able** _____	12. inscrut**able** _____
3. inexor**able** _____	13. insuper**able** _____
4. inevit**able** _____	14. indomit**able** _____
5. memor**able** _____	15. malle**able** _____
6. prob**able** _____	16. vulner**able** _____
7. unconscion**able** ___	17. aff**able** _____
8. port**able** _____	18. palp**able** _____
9. ar**able** _____	19. culp**able** _____
10. ineff**able** _____	

12. That, on the other hand, *-ible* attaches to most *non-word* roots.

aud**ible** _____ divis**ible** _____

etc.

13. That *-ible* attaches to full-word roots that have an immediate *-ion* form.

digest**ible** _____ corrupt**ible** _____

etc.

14. That the exceptions to Statement 13 are:

predict**able** _____ correct**able** _____
detect**able** _____

15. That *-ible* attaches to roots ending in *-ns* or *-miss*.

comprehens**ible** _____ admiss**ible** _____

etc.

16. That the important exceptions to Statement 15 are:

dispens**able** _____ indispens**able** _____

17. That *-ible* attaches to roots ending in soft *-g* or soft *-c*.

invinc**ible** _____ intang**ible** _____

etc.

18. That Statement 17 excludes the special *-able* words in which a softening *-e* is retained after *-g* or *-c*.

service**able** _____ manage**able** _____

etc.

19. And that, finally, *-ible* attaches to eight special roots which have no common characteristics. These are:

contempt**ible** _____ collaps**ible** _____
gull**ible** _____ resist**ible** _____
flex**ible** _____ irresist**ible** _____
inflex**ible** _____ discern**ible** _____

243

As to the problem of -er or -or, you have learned:

20. That mistakes are rarely made in words that end in -er; therefore, when in doubt, you are probably safe in using the -or ending.

21. That otherwise you must rely on your kinesthetic and visual memory, as no general principle effectively separates the chaff from the wheat—or the lambs from the goats.

FOURTH REVIEW TEST

I. Decide whether -ance or -ence attaches to each root, then rewrite the complete word.

1. refer— _____ (ence)
2. resist— _____ (ance)
3. persever— _____ (ance)
4. occurr— _____ (ence)
5. transfer— _____ (ence)
6. admitt— _____ (ance)
7. deliver— _____ (ance)
8. confid— _____ (ence)
9. exist— _____ (ence)
10. mainten— _____ (ance)
11. abund— _____ (ance)
12. irrelev— _____ (ance)

II. Decide whether -ery or -ary attaches to each root, then rewrite the complete word.

1. secret— _____ (ary)
2. monast— _____ (ery)
3. millin— _____ (ery)
4. confection— _____ (ery)
5. cemet— _____ (ery)
6. dysent— _____ (ery)
7. diction— _____ (ary)

III. Decide whether *-able* or *-ible* attaches to each root, then rewrite the complete word.

(Full words)

1. detest— _____ (able)
2. depend— _____ (able)
3. accept— _____ (able)

(Full words lacking *-e*)

4. deplor— _____ (able)
5. excit— _____ (able)

(*i* ending)

6. envi— _____ (able)
7. soci— _____ (able)

(Other forms with *-a*)

8. irrit— _____ (able)
9. inimit— _____ (able)
10. abomin— _____ (able)

(Hard *c* or *g*)

11. despic— _____ (able)
12. indefatig— _____ (able)

(Non-words)

13. compat— _____ (ible)
14. feas— _____ (ible)
15. plaus— _____ (ible)
16. combust— _____ (ible)
17. infall— _____ (ible)
18. suscept— _____ (ible)

(Full words with immediate -ion forms)

19. collect— _____ (ible)
20. digest— _____ (ible)
21. corrupt— _____ (ible)
22. connect— _____ (ible)
23. perfect— _____ (ible)
24. suggest— _____ (ible)

(Exceptions to above)

25. predict— _____ (able)
26. detect— _____ (able)

27. correct— _____ (able)

(Root ends in *-ns* or *-miss*)

28. defens— _____ (ible)

29. admiss— _____ (ible)

30. incomprehens— _____ (ible)

31. permiss— _____ (ible)

(Exception to above)

32. indispens— _____ (able)

(Soft *-c* or *-g*)

33. invinc— _____ (ible)

34. forc— _____ (ible)

35. neglig— _____ (ible)

36. irreduc— _____ (ible)

(Artificially softened *-c* or *-g*)

37. enforce— _____ (able)

38. notice— _____ (able)

39. charge— _____ (able)

40. manage— _____ (able)

(Special exceptions)

41. equit— _____ (able)

42. insuper— _____ (able)

43. vulner— _____ (able)

44. formid— _____ (able)

45. culp— _____ (able)

46. contempt— _____ (ible)

47. collaps— _____ (ible)

48. irresist— _____ (ible)

IV. Decide whether *-er* or *-or* attaches to each root, then rewrite the complete word.

1. commentat— _____ (or)

2. elevat— _____ (or)

3. visit— _____ (or)

4. investigat— _____ (or)

5. surviv— _____ (or)

32

How to Avoid British and Other Ostentatious Spellings

PROBLEMS

hon**our** or hon**or**?
glam**our** or glam**or**?
aesthetic or **e**sthetic?
che**que** or che**ck**?

SOLUTION

American spelling is sufficiently illogical, contradictory, ironic, and uncontrollable without our going out of our way to make it even more so.

Of this I am sure you are now convinced, if indeed you did not have that conviction long before you picked up this book.

Efforts have been made for years to simplify our patterns and combinations, and I am sorry to have to tell you that very little progress can be reported. Attempts to make such pronunciation-spellings as *laf* (laugh), *fotograf* (photograph), *hed* (head), *nife* (knife), *activ* (active), *dout* (doubt), and *tuf* (tough) acceptable and popular have met with the most ignominious failure, as you can appreciate—yet some forward steps have been taken and it would be only the most die-hard and obstinate reactionary who would refuse to accept those comparatively new and logical patterns which are now in widespread and preferable use.

For example, Column I shows former spellings which have almost universally given way to the modern forms in Column II.

I. Old Spellings	II. Modern Forms
aesthetic	esthetic
aeroplane	airplane[1]
aeon	eon
oesophagus	esophagus
encyclopaedia	encyclopedia
mediaeval	medieval
foetus	fetus
anaemia	anemia
programme	program
quartette	quartet
centre	center
metre	meter
calibre	caliber
fibre	fiber
manoeuvre	maneuver
theatre	theater
mould	mold
moult	molt

Most of these older spellings are particularly popular in England, and there are Britons who sneer at our simpler forms—the fact remains, nevertheless, that in American spelling the modern combinations are not only preferable but almost universally found in all writing of however formal a character.

(A few words, despite their illogical and old-fashioned appearance hold on tenaciously to popular fancy in America—for example, the older form *gauge* is more

---

[1]There are those fence-sitters who compromise by writing *airoplane*—but this bastardized pattern, I am happy to report, has no sanction whatever.

prevalent than the modern *gage*, and *aerial* is still the only permissible pattern.)

British spelling is in many instances different, almost startlingly so, from American patterns, and usually more complicated, and it would be unwise and conspicuous, to say the least, if not actually ostentatious, to become too thoroughly addicted to British forms.

In England, for example, the *-our* ending is prevalent: *honour, labour, behaviour, demeanour, humour, flavour, neighbour,* etc. American style always drops the unnecessary *-u*, preferring *honor, labor, behavior, demeanor, humor, flavor, neighbor,* etc.

(*Glamour*, however, is the preferable American spelling, perhaps because it has a certain air about it—but the adjective is correctly written *glamorous.*)

British spelling tends to use an *-yse* or *-ise* ending when we prefer *-yze* and *-ize*—Englishmen will write *analyse, paralyse, civilise, apologise,* etc., for our *analyze, paralyze, civilize, apologize,* etc. And Britons prefer *kerb* to *curb, tyre* to *tire, gaol* to *jail, enquiry* to *inquiry, storey* to *story* (for the floors of a building), *cheque* to *check,* and *racquet* to *racket* (that is, in tennis or badminton—our *racket* as an illegal enterprise or a great noise is also the British spelling).

In England *plough* is written for *plow; defence, offence,* and *pretence* for *defense, offense,* and *pretense,* and *connexion, inflexion,* and *reflexion* for *connection, inflection* and *reflection.* (But *complexion* is the only acceptable form on both sides of the ocean.)

There is also the British tendency to double a consonant in verb forms where we prefer to leave it alone— *cancelled, traveller, travelled, jeweller, jewelled,* etc. American preference is for the single *-l* in these and similar words—indeed American preference is always for the simpler, closer-to-pronunciation spelling.

You are always safer using the simpler, American pattern in any word—British spelling may give an interesting continental air to your writing but it will also invest it with a stiff and unfamiliar appearance.

How far can you go in simplifying your spelling? You have probably seen *thru, tho, altho, thoro, thoroly, nite* and *thot* (*thought*) in informal communications—and for such writing these may be acceptable to a degree. In any kind of business or formal letters they are considered out of place. It is true that they may show a refreshing freedom from conventional spelling habits rather than ignorance, but when you spell correctly you give up your right to freedom and have to accept almost complete conformity to rules and custom, which is all that English spelling generally is.

Unless you agree with that notoriously poor speller, Andrew Jackson, our seventh President, who, you recall, claimed that "It is a dammed poor mind that can think of only one way to spell a word."

According to one story, which may or may not be authentic but which makes awfully good telling, President Jackson originated the phrase "O.K." When government documents came to his desk, so the story goes, he would read them through and if he found them in proper order he would scrawl O.K. at the bottom and initial them. Why O.K.? Well, it's perfectly simple— Jackson was abbreviating *all correct,* which he spelled *"orl korrect"!*

So maybe the "dammed poor mind" attitude was a thinly veiled excuse for ignorance rather than a courageous expression of healthy rebellion. . . .

33

How to Continue Your Improvement in Spelling

The training program you have just finished—

Has given you mastery over the important basic principles of English spelling—

Has probably eliminated most of your *unconscious* errors—

Has developed in you complete and perhaps automatic control over the kinds of words commonly and consistently misspelled by the average literate person—

Has sharpened your visual and kinesthetic memory of the correct patterns of these words to such a degree that you can now spell them not only without error but also without doubts, misgivings, or hesitation—

Has eliminated the causes of any insecurity or confusion about the proper forms of troublesome demons—

Has helped you come to terms with the contradictions, complexities, paradoxes and inconsistencies of the system of spelling under which we operate—

Has made you, if you have worked carefully and conscientiously, a competent, self-assured, and perhaps near-perfect speller.

This program has probably eliminated close to 98 per cent of the errors you have been in the habit of making or were likely to make.

For further improvement, if there happens to be room

for such improvement, you need to discover the special, uncommon, it may be *unconscious*, errors not covered by your training.

It is possible that a small number of words (in the average case no more than a dozen or so) are your pet demons—words which you (and practically no one else) misspells.

With the alertness to error that your training has developed in you, you will soon discover such unique errors, if they exist.

Then your skill in visual, kinesthetic, and mnemonic responses to correct patterns will stand you in good stead.

For you now know how to locate the crucial area of any word you misspell—

How to make a complete visual and kinesthetic adjustment to its proper form—

And how to develop a mnemonic for any demon which is particularly troublesome.

In a sense, there is little need to tell you these things.

For, if the intensive training offered in this book has been successful in your case, you will discover and eliminate any further or unique errors not covered by this program—and you will do so without any urging on my part.

You will remain for quite a time visually alert to the appearance in your reading of all the words on which you have trained.

And you will probably discover more errors in printed material, as a result of your training and alertness, than you ever realized existed.

You will then appreciate how nearly expert you have become, how long a stride toward perfection you have taken, how rare an ability you have begun to develop.

Index

Index

Index

Index

dys-, 55–56
Dysentery, 56, 210
Dyspeptic, 56

-e rules
  exceptions to dropped *e*
    rules, 113–117
  when to drop final *e*,
    82–85, 113–117
  when to keep *e* after *c*,
    94–97
  when to keep *c* after *g*,
    102–107
Eavesdropping, 185
Ecstasy, 135
Edible, 227
Educable, 223
Educator, 239
Efficient, 74
ei and *ie see ie* and *ei*
Either, 67
Elevator, 239
Eligible, 231
Embarrassed, 16, 60, 61
Embraceable, 95, 231
Emphatically, 126
-ence or *-ance*, 34, 196–199
Encouragement, 105
Encyclopedia, 248
Enforceable, 97, 231
Enfranchise, 42
Engageable, 104, 231
Engagement, 105
English spelling *see* British
  spelling
Enrageable, 231
Enterprise, 41
Enveloped, 173
Envelopment, 114, 175
Enviable, 222
Eon, 248

Equipment, 114, 174
Equipped, 172
Equitable, 225
-er or *-or*, 228–229, 238
Errors
  constantly recurring, 14
  unconscious, 13
-ery or *-ary*, 209–211
Escalator, 239
Esophagus, 248
Esthetic, 248
Estimable, 223
Evidently, 124
Exceed, 27, 28
Excelled, 173
Excellence, 184
Excellent, 184
Exceptions, 15
Excise, 41
Excitable, 221, 228
Exercise, 41
Exhaustible, 229
Exhilarate, 87
Existence, 200
Exorcise, 41
Expansible, 229, 230
Expectable, 228
Experimentally, 125
Explicable, 223
Extravagance, 199
Eyeing or eying, 115

Fabricator, 239
Fahrenheit, 68
Feasible, 227
Fetus, 248
Fiber, 248
Field, 65
Fiend, 65, 68
Financier, 66
Finite, 213

258

Index

Index

Index

Index

There's an epidemic with 27 million victims. And no visible symptoms.

It's an epidemic of people who can't read.

Believe it or not, 27 million Americans are functionally illiterate, about one adult in five.

The solution to this problem is you... when you join the fight against illiteracy. So call the Coalition for Literacy at toll-free **1-800-228-8813** and volunteer.

Volunteer Against Illiteracy. The only degree you need is a degree of caring.